Raw STAR Recipes

ORGANIC MEALS, SNACKS & DESSERTS IN 10 MINUTES

ECO CHEF BRYAN AU

Eco Chef Bryan Au Raw Star Recipes: Organic Meals, Snacks & Desserts Under 10 Minutes

By Eco Chef Bryan Au

E-mail: rawbryan@hotmail.com
Website: www.EcoChefApp.com Or www.RawInTenMinutes.com

Art Direction and Design: Matt O'Leary
Food Photography and Styling by: Bryan Au
Portrait Photography by: Anett Braley

Published by FastPencil Premiere
an imprint of FastPencil, Inc.
3131 Bascom Ave. Suite 150 • Campbell CA 95008 USA
(408) 540-7571 • (408) 540-7572 (Fax) • info@fastpencil.com
http://premiere.fastpencil.com

ISBN 9781607463962

I dedicate this book to everyone and the entire planet
because I love you all and I hope you enjoy
my recipes for the best in health and happiness.

CONTENTS

INTRODUCTION

It is the healing, loving intention of this book to present Raw Organic Cuisine, Snacks and Desserts as one of the most important and best new foods in modern times: unique, gourmet, and the ultimate in health food. Celebrity Eco Chef Bryan Au blends an international menu of everyone's favorite foods, including "junk food" and comfort food, with the finest in new, healthy, raw organic recipes for you to enjoy. This cookbook is a culmination of twelve plus years of Chef Bryan Au's world travels, learning, experimenting and perfecting the new level of Raw Organic Food so popular today.

Millions of people are discovering the incredible tastes, flavors and health that come from eating RAW food and living this way. The effects are instantaneous, you can feel the new energy and amazing quality in each recipe. Vibrant tastes and new flavors await, to be discovered and enjoyed in the RAW, with an international menu spanning: American, Italian, Mexican, Chinese, Spanish, Japanese, Thai, Indian, Mediterranean and Vietnamese cuisine.

In the 1970s, Raw Organic Food, as it was called, was mostly underground, enjoyed by free thinkers and health seekers. Eating RAW quickly became a lifestyle and food trend well into the 1990s as more people discovered its all natural effects, including anti-aging, prevention of disease, and reversal of many conditions such as cancer, diabetes, and obesity.

It has been Hollywood's best kept beauty secret, with many famous actors and actresses reportedly embracing the Raw Food Diet, as it was called. Actress Demi Moore did it for Charlie's Angels II, and everyone marveled at how young, slim and amazing she looked. Supermodel Carol Alt authored two best selling books about how RAW organic food saved her health and career. Major media reports of Sting, Donna Karan, Forest Whitaker, Lisa Bonet, Alicia Silverstone, Woody Harrelson, Cher and many more reveal the benefits of RAW food.

Meanwhile, Celebrity Eco Chef Bryan Au was busy promoting and creating the best raw organic food with fast, fun and simple raw organic recipes that looked and tasted like everyone's favorite "junk food" and comfort foods. He has expanded to: Raw Organic restaurants, an organic ingredients & snack foodline, Eco Organic fashions, DVDs, TV shows, media appearances and much more. Now you are holding in your hands Chef Bryan Au's best recipe inventions.

This new book is about empowering you to make and enjoy RAW Organic Food in an ultra gourmet, light, rejuvenating and refreshing way. Although the recipes are so easy that kids can make them safely with supervision, they are for everyone to make and enjoy, from kids, teenagers and college students to parents, families and seniors. Emphasis is placed on gourmet presentation, super health benefits and gourmet flavor. With the exception of a few new dehydrated recipes that are innovative and amazing, most recipes in this book are all fresh, and can be prepared in less than 10 minutes. Eco Chef Bryan Au once again makes his techniques and recipes accessible, simple, easy, fast, fun and delicious!

You will also find dishes inspired by more traditional spa cuisine, such as seafood, soups, sauces, and the use of tropical fruits. All the recipes in this book are 100% vegan, organic and RAW, but they look and taste cooked, baked or deep fried. The

words "vegan," "raw," and "organic" now have become desirable, practical and fashionable. Major popular celebrities that you have seen and heard of in the media are proving that eating vegan is a beneficial health trend. You will discover that these vegan recipes are more creamy, delicious and amazing than any other foods you have tried!

Each recipe is deliciously easy, simple, fast and fun to make. They are safe for children to make with supervision, because there is no cooking involved and the recipes are all natural. Parents can enjoy quality time with their kids while creating fabulously healthy nutritious meals. You don't need a personal chef or special restaurant to get these special treats. Now you can easily and quickly make them yourself, at home or anywhere! Well researched and based on the advice, recommendations and books of Gabriel Cousens, M.D., these recipes are not only delicious, but provide benefits for anti-aging as well as optimal peak performance. RAW and vegan foods are eco green, environmentally friendly and good for you

and the planet. I want to empower you to be the Raw Star! We are all here to help and support each other and enjoy the best in health together.

Let's have fun and enjoy the next level of health with Celebrity Eco Chef Bryan Au's special new recipes and techniques. These recipes will also help to prevent and reverse obesity, diabetes and cancer in the most all natural ways possible. Some famous recipes revealed in this book: 5 Minute Chocolate Cake, Pancakes, Mango "Cheesecake," Spanish Lasagna, the all new "Pepperoni" Pizza, "Beef" Stir Fry and Fruit Danish. Ice creams, soups, entrees, cookies, cakes, pies and more are waiting for you to discover, so join in the popular Raw Organic Adventure!

ABOUT BRYAN AU

Hi! I am Eco Chef Bryan Au. My goal is to create more access, education and awareness about Raw Organic Gourmet Cuisine, Snacks and Desserts, and how eating in this way can improve the health of people and the planet. It has been proven recently that our very food choices have the greatest carbon foot print and affect global warming, and consequently our well being and that of the entire world. Why not choose the most healthy and fun recipes, which can literally help to solve everything?

With my fun, healthy recipes, you can save your: money, health, community and the environment. My new motto is "Save Everything!" Now you can, in the most fun, fashionable and delicious ways possible.

You truly can become the Raw Star, and a superhero in the world! It is so easy to choose something that is incredibly nutritious and healthy. Each person is more powerful than they realize. It all starts with each individual decision, and the great transformation is already happening. I see it every day in the media and around the world. I would like people to know about the very real Raw Organic and Eco choices available, and to see how much happiness, joy and vitality these choices will add to their lives. I have seen how people blossom into natural leaders and educators, who then help spread knowledge and education to others so that all can benefit. This is my healing mission and path in life. I also want to create opportunities, jobs and a entirely new eco green industry.

People ask how I became a Raw Organic Chef. My journey has taken me to Hawaii, Cancun, Puerto Vallarta, Thailand, to ancient temples deep in the jungles of Bourabadour on Java Island and in Bali, to London, England and to Venice, Italy. I have toured Europe, Asia, the Bahamas, Mexico, most of the 50 United States of America, Tokyo, Japan and Canada. I love Hawaii, Los Angeles and New York. I have studied with holistic and alternative doctors, Chinese medicine doctors, Ayurvedic doctors and cutting edge organic gourmet raw food chefs. While keeping up with the latest nutrition principles, I have published articles about yoga, exhibited at art shows, and made films and videos promoting charities and fundraisers for great causes.

Through Raw Organic Cuisine I am manifesting the true spirit of love, joy and compassion as my contribution to healing people and the world. I hope you fully enjoy my recipes in the most healing and healthiest way possible! I engage in constant study of modern

ABOUT BRYAN AU

principles of nutrition and healing from a vast source of experts, most notably Gabriel Cousens, M.D. As the world's foremost live foods medical doctor, he has authored many well regarded books, which I highly recommend. My recipes are based on his incredible research.

As a RAW Organic Chef, I create the most decadent gourmet creations as well as all the homestyle comfort food and "junk food" favorites, with all the added benefits of being raw and organic. "Raw" just means that it is all natural and not cooked, baked or deep fried. This helps to maintain a raw, organic, all natural eco green lifestyle. I call this Eco Green Cuisine because we are not using fossil fuels while minimizing our carbon footprint and not creating pollution. Instead we are becoming part of the healthy solution!

I am appealing to all the comforts and memories associated with food, so it is not all celery sticks and "twigs," as people may think, nor is it just sushi or salads either. It is the most enjoyable, delicious and amazing gourmet cuisine possible on Earth! It has led me on great adventures, meeting the most incredible and gifted people while increasing my health and happiness. I created this book so that I can share all this goodness with you.

I have became convinced, based on my findings and from people I have met, that this is indeed the most optimal and incredible diet and cuisine in existence. The best way to judge this is by eating it. Right away you can tell the difference in the gourmet taste, in your energy levels, and in your feeling of satisfaction with the delicious assortment of new creative flavors to choose from. I found I was able to transform and tap into amazing creative, artistic abilities that I didn't even know I had. Raw Organic food allows you to flow into more spontaneous joy and creativity, and greater connections occur in your life. It opens you up to an amazing new journey and adventure of discovery.

I have found Gabriel Cousens to be the most incredible author, healer and physician on the face of the planet, and many agree with me. I highly suggest that you explore his books. They have changed my life for the better, and since that time I have been on the adventure of love and learning of a lifetime. Eating RAW helps to solve obesity, diabetes, cancer and many modern day conditions. You can find many incredible personal testimonials, medical research and more online.

This book is the culmination of my entire life learning and experiences so far. All of my heart, soul and love are literally embedded within each page and recipe of this book. My recipes incorporate sound health principles. I take out the guesswork by providing the best, most well researched recipes for you to enjoy. They all take 10 minutes or less to make, some are even just 5 or 2 minutes! But the point is to enjoy making these recipes. It is not a race against the clock, so please take your time in making them and do not rush through the recipes. If you can't make them in under 10 minutes, that is perfectly fine too. They are still very quick, fun and easy. With practice, you will find that they really are under 10 minutes to make. I hope you can teach others and share the food with loved ones as well. I truly want people to discover this new incredible way of eating, living and thinking. I know you will love it as much as the millions of people who have already discovered its benefits for themselves.

Currently I am a personal trainer, Organic Raw food chef, yoga instructor, healer, artist, Eco Green Expert and Consultant, peace activist and more! I have worked with celebrity clients like Alicia Silverstone and Lisa Bonet. I have clients who are CEOs, dancers, artists, healers, and everyone who is interested in the most vibrant health and food on the planet.

It is an honor and joy for me to share the best recipes I have created for you. Life is an adventure, and eating Raw organic will lead you to greater things in life. Health is the ultimate wealth. I always tell people that eating Raw will give you more energy and open your mind to higher truths so that you can share them with others with support and healing, and just love one another in the best ways possible.

Thank you for joining in the new RAW organic all natural healthy adventure,

Eco Chef Bryan Au
www.RawInTenMinutes.com

CHAPTER ONE

One of the main points of Raw Organic Cuisine is the fact that every ingredient is 100% Organic and Raw. Being Organic puts this cuisine above the rest, simply because it is so pure and natural. Our bodies are also 100% Raw and Organic, so it makes perfect sense that we consume the same thing. The effects of organic fruit and vegetables are healing for people and for the planet. This is what attracted me to this amazing, special cuisine at the beginning. You will discover that it allows for so much creativity and joy in your life too. I look forward to creating new recipes every day.

It is such a rewarding and fun experience for me to create new, awesome recipes for people to enjoy. We even have some new fun words like RAWesome, which is Raw and Awesome put together. I urge you to research supporting and consuming Organic food and products, one of the most valuable practices to maintain our bodies and our Earth. With that said, ALL of the ingredients in this Recipe Book are 100% Organic and RAW. I want to state that because I did not type Organic and Raw in front of each and every ingredient, but do want to emphasize this important aspect of Raw Organic Cuisine.

Sometimes this very important Organic concept is overlooked when it should be emphasized. There really is a difference! When you eat more Organic food, you will notice how much better you feel, and you won't want to go back to processed or inorganic food. When people say that Organic is too expensive, I tell them they are worth it. There are no pesticides used in the food, the water is pure, and the land and workers are protected. There are strict, beneficial standards to meet for food to be certified Organic. The truth is, all the goodness they receive in health and in saving the Earth is worth the slight extra cost.

The more we support Organic fruits and vegetables, the more mainstream and profitable it will become, allowing prices to go down for all of us. That is why I try my best to promote Organic and Raw living foods; I would like them to be normal and mainstream again. Not too long ago, food was all natural and organic, and did not require a label to make it so. Times have changed, but one day I hope that we can return to that natural state of being and living. The intent of this book is to introduce new people to this wonderful new cuisine and to offer the people who already enjoy it with the best Raw recipes in the world.

Everyone will love how fast and easy these under 10 minutes recipes are. Most are under $10 as well. Only a few of the recipes involve dehydrating using a Good4U Dehydrator, which takes longer than 10 minutes to complete. However, the recipes are still 10 minutes or less to make before having to dehydrate for about 10-12 hours. The rest of the recipes are all fresh, raw and simple to make, yet appear quite gourmet and fancy, as if you spent hours making them!

Raw Organic Cuisine is really taking off. There are movies like Woody Harrelson's Go Further, which I recommended that you see and support, and more exciting, vibrant Raw Organic products, books and restaurants popping up everywhere. This is such a beautiful trend, currently the number one growing industry in America. Thank you for joining in the adventure! I hope you truly enjoy all of my recipes.

Next, the difference between Raw and Living Foods. Raw foods are those that are not cooked and in their natural state. Living foods are still alive, growing and vibrant. Living foods can be put into the earth and a plant or tree will grow as a result. Raw food can be sundried or dehydrated; few of my recipes use dehydration. Living and Raw foods will not lose any active enzymes or nutrients while adding water and hydration to your body. Our bodies are more than 80% water, so the more pure water you drink or get from food, the healthier you will become. My recipes are tantalizingly juicy and moist, helping to keep you hydrated and at peak performance levels while still super delicious and gourmet.

Some examples of living foods: sprouts, fruit, and nuts that are soaked overnight (one of the few things that take prep time). Soaking is simple and easy, "soaked" in front of an ingredient or item means to soak that ingredient overnight, with water bottled in glass, in a large covered bowl or container in a clean dry area. This will turn Raw food into Living food alive with enzymes and life force with living nutrients.

Enzymes are the building blocks of life and the secret to the fountain of youth. Because many of the recipes are blended raw organic or living foods, it actually takes less enzymes to digest as well so they save the amount of work and energy that your body uses. Other types of foods or cuisines require more work, energy and enzymes for your body to break down, which can deplete you or cause disease.

Raw Living foods have the highest amount of enzymes possible. By eating these foods, you increase the amount of enzymes in your body, which help increase your energy levels, provide natural anti-aging and give you strength. By soaking ingredients and using sprouts and miso, along with other techniques incorporated into my recipes, you will be able to deliciously enjoy all the super benefits without even realizing it, and become superheroes! Exciting research and discoveries are happening every day, so it is important to be up-to-date with information. New information and research has been done recently that other recipe books may not have incorporated. This is what makes my recipes so special. You can be assured that you are getting the best.

So, we can convert Raw foods into Living foods by soaking them in pure water overnight and allowing them to sprout or be activated. Some items only require a few minutes of soaking (specified in each recipe), such as goji berries or sundried tomatoes. If the ingredient is marked "soaked," it means simply soaking it overnight before you go to bed. You may also soak the same ingredients for another day or two if you want them sprouted; this requires only rinsing often, changing the water, and ensuring a dry, clean area for the duration. In these recipes, you may choose to use the nuts Raw or to use them Living, by soaking them in pure water overnight, which makes them easier to digest. You can use Raw or Living nuts interchangeably, remembering that soaked nuts are wetter in consistency and should be drained and rinsed thoroughly before adding to the recipe.

Now I would like to describe the equipment that you will need to make these recipes and the ingredients that we will use often throughout the book. I have designed these recipes to be the quickest, most economical and fastest possible, with the most gourmet and decadent flavors, accessible for the total beginner and also the Raw expert. We will mainly use a blender, measuring cups, a sharp knife (I recommend my new RAW STAR Ceramic Knives), a vegetable grater, a peeler and cheesecloth. You may use a food processor for some recipes, if you want the consistency of certain ingredients to be finer or powdered.

A word about blenders. You can use any blender, but I have found that it is worth it to save for a professional, high powered blender. I use and recommend the Blendtec blender, which makes the food deliciously smooth, creamy, more enjoyable and very easy to digest. It is also a fun piece of equipment to use! I encourage you to think about investing in the best blender possible that is heavy duty and will last a long time. Cheap or inexpensive blenders may seem to be a good value but they are not strong enough and often times break down and have to be replaced. Getting the best blender will ensure a longer lasting high performance blender and the quality will show up in your food preparation. Saving for a high quality professional blender will actually save you time and money in the long run. Many people have confirmed this fact so I want to share it with you.

A Blendtec blender pays off because it makes the food easier and more fun to prepare, allowing creativity to come through without the struggles and hassles found in other blenders. Of all the blenders in all the different kitchens that I have used, I prefer and can only recommend the Blendtec, the "Rolls Royce" of blenders, the best in quality, design, craftsmanship. They are smooth, computerized with nicely lit digital LCD displays and easy to use, soft push buttons. They have a strong, three horsepower motor with sturdy blades made of high quality aircraft grade stainless steel. Their containers are light and easy to clean; food does not hide or get stuck behind the specially designed blades as it does in other blenders. Many professional restaurants and gourmet kitchens use them as well. Their home kitchen series is very similar and comparable to the professional industrial series. I recommend the Blendtec Blender and have found a special discounted source for your orders on my website.

If you are going to make a lot of food, run a restaurant or catering business, I recommend ordering extra blender jars so you will almost have two blenders in one. You can interchange them and not have to wait and to wash one after each use. I actually have 3 jars for each blender, allowing me to make an entrée, soup, smoothie or dessert very quickly without taking time to wash the jar after each use, which saves time and is a great tip.

Other equipment includes measuring cups, a vegetable mandolin, a grater, peeler and cheesecloth, which you can buy at any kitchen supply or department store.

For the Raw Organic ingredients I recommend your local Organic Farmer's Markets, as they have the freshest and best selections. You can get to know the farmers on a personal level and get great discounts! Organic farmers are providing a great service by taking the extra time and cost to lovingly offer us the best that nature and God have to offer. They deserve our support, plus it is just fun to shop at Farmer's Markets.

Not everyone has access to a Organic Farmer's Market, and they are not always open around the clock or year round, so I often shop at Whole Foods Market, Trader Joe's and local health food stores and co-ops. I love Trader Joe's prices and their selection of Raw Organic fruit and nuts. They have great deals and make a serious effort to carry Organic products, so we can support their noble efforts. Whole Foods Market is pretty awesome for Organic foods too, with good quality selections and many locations. Again, the more we support Organic products, the more profits these stores can make, allowing their buyers to order more Organic selections, and soon the prices become better for everyone and it becomes a winning, self-sustaining situation. Even regular supermarkets are beginning to carry more Organics, to make it easy for you to buy more Organic! The more you practice this, the more other companies will have to transform and cater to our needs. We can make a positive difference and each choice we make really counts. I personally buy only Organic and environmental products. It makes me feel good, supporting people and companies that are really doing it right. I also love the fact that they provide me with the opportunity to treat myself to the best in Organic foods for the benefit of my health and well being, the environment and the world.

Now, for the ingredients we will use the most in this book. I will explain their benefits and introduce new superfoods such as Organic Tibetan goji berries, which have the highest amounts of antioxidants and vitamin C and are full of super goodness. They also have a wonderful natural happiness inducing quality about them. Whenever I eat a handful, I feel energized and happy. Goji berries really work!

There are many ingredients that I will not use and others that I promote fully. I have found that most people do not really like to be told what they can and can't eat, so I recommend reading Gabriel Cousens' books for true medical, scientific and spiritual information about Raw Organic Cuisine. I am so thankful for Gabriel's research and contributions to the world, I even e-mailed the Nobel Committee in Switzerland to nominate him for a Noble Prize! I feel that his achievements and contributions to the world are that great. I will leave it to his expertise to explain which ingredients to avoid and which to use. Just know that while I have done the best research possible to bring you the fastest, most gourmet and enjoyable RAW Recipes in less than 10 minutes and under $10, these recipes are also the most balanced and the best for your health.

The under 10 minute concept is not a race or requirement, but an estimate of how long these recipes take to make. The number one thing is to be able to enjoy the experience while being safe. I want you to enjoy the process and not rush or hurry to make that 10 minute mark! If you take your time, you will find preparing these recipes to be fun, rewarding and relaxing. For me it is like a meditation and total zen experience, being in the moment, fully concentrating and enjoying what I am doing, knowing that I am preparing the best food possible on the planet!

This is the way we ate for millions of years and the way nature intended. All of the six billion living beings on Earth eat and thrive on Raw Organic food. This is an interesting figure and definite food for thought. We are only now starting to learn more from nature's wisdom and rediscovering natural healing and lifestyle choices. This is why we must become more environmentally conscious and protect the same nature that provides for our needs so abundantly.

A few recipes may exceed the $10 mark, but most are well under $10. Recipes are created to serve 1-2 people; I will specifically state if a recipe serves more, so you will know that you'll have extra servings. It is always good to have some extra Raw Organic food on hand in the refrigerator so you can just reach in there and enjoy it later, or to share with friends and family. You can, of course, double or triple the recipes if you have more guests or people to serve.

ALL of these recipes should be eaten and served right away for the maximum amount of freshness and nutrients, but in case of leftovers, please cover and refrigerate right away to protect vital nutrients, as you would with all foods. Most of the food will last several days to one week maximum in the refrigerator. Please use your common sense and compost the food if you suspect that it is no longer fresh. You will find that some of the Raw Organic food tastes better with time because the ingredients and flavors get a chance to meld, mix and merge for even more flavor. But for the maximum amount of energy, enzymes and nutrients, try to eat it right after preparing. I like to use glassware for storage because they are sturdy, attractive and easy to use. I buy them at different kitchen or retail stores.

Please carefully wash *everything* well before preparing recipes: your hands, produce, all equipment, utensils, plates, kitchen counters, etc. Wash your hands often before and during food preparation, using all natural organic eco soaps and cleansers such as the Seventh Generation brand or similar ecologically conscious products with biodegradable packaging. Each choice you make really does affect seven generations into the future! Let's make collective decisions that make our future brighter with awareness and positive choices.

You will totally amaze your friends and family with incredible creations from these following recipes. Even the complete beginner with little skill in the kitchen will be able to astonish hungry guests!

Back to the ingredients, listed below in order of most frequent use in the recipes. Ensure that your purchases say RAW and Organic on the produce, label, jar, bulk bin, etc. Again, you can find these ingredients at Farmer's Markets, Whole Foods, Trader Joe's or your local health food store or co-op.

PINE NUTS: I like these because of their creamy, smooth flavor and their small size, which makes them easy to blend. They come from pine cones! Pine nuts make the best creams and sauces and are also great whole. I sometimes will mix them with Goji Berries for an instant superfood trail mix. Pine Nuts at a good price can be found at Trader Joe's or at Whole Foods, where they are found in the bulk section. Make sure they say Raw Organic! Trader Joe's pine nuts are individually packed to retain great fresh flavor. If you can find them fresher at a Farmer's Market, then I would say go for that! Always try to taste them first to see how fresh and good they are. Each crop is different, and you want the best.

BRAZIL NUTS: These only grow in the rainforest and have amazing healing properties. I have found that they make excellent Alfredo Sauces and work well in some desserts too. You may substitute brazil nuts in recipes that call for pine nuts and vice versa. Experiment to keep things fresh, new and exciting.

ALMONDS: These should definitely be sprouted and soaked overnight in the most pure water you can find. They have so many health benefits, and more are being discovered each day! You will make Almond Milk and can also use the leftover almond pulp in many recipes, so it is important to get some good quality, all natural cheesecloth. You can drink the almond milk or store it in glass jars for later use. The pulp can be used right away or be stored in glass Pyrex containers in the refrigerator. The Almond Milk recipe is in the Raw Oatmeal and Cereal recipe. I found information online that states that raw almonds have healthy fats, have been found to help reduce heart disease, and help weight loss when people are on low calorie diets that include raw almonds. Almonds are high in antioxidants such as Vitamin E, and high in magnesium.

SUNFLOWER SEEDS: These are the most affordable of all the Raw Organic nuts. They are easy to blend because of their small size, and can be used in place of other nuts in some recipes. Sunflower seeds can be soaked overnight and sprouted before use. They are very versatile, and also happen to make the best sprouts. I love the way they taste and how their small goodness comes from giant, beautiful flowers.

OLIVE OIL: I use this special ingredient in most recipes because of its great flavor and energy and for natural health reasons. There are many different types of Organic olive oils on the market today.

SUNFLOWER SPROUTS: Gabriel Cousens says that sprouts are one of the best Raw Living foods you can eat, and I believe him. Sprouts contain vital living enzymes and nutrients, and yes, they are still growing! I prefer sunflower sprouts because of their flavor and presentation, and because they are so thick that they last longer than other sprouts. I use these versatile Living superfoods in many recipes, as they go well with most foods and recipes, taste great, and people love them. I buy them already sprouted for convenience, but you can easily sprout them yourself in several days. There are many ready made sprouting kits and information online. Sprouting is a rewarding experience that will connect you with the miracle of Living foods and the forces of life.

KELP GRANULES WITH CAYENNE PEPPER: Kelp granules supply your body with all the minerals it needs and craves. Ayurvedic medicine states that cayenne pepper both activates the digestive system and promotes healthy digestion. It also adds a nice spicy flavor and "heat" to the food. On a cold day or during the winter, you may want to use more cayenne pepper in your food. I use it in most of my recipes, but it is optional; adjust according to your liking of spiciness. Maine Sea Vegetable Company makes a premixed package that is a good price and quality.

MISO MASTER ORGANIC CHICKPEA MISO: I use miso in my recipes due to Gabriel Cousens' recommendation to use miso rather than other traditional salty soy products. Gabriel gives an in depth explanation in his new amazing book, Rainbow Green Live Food Cuisine, a recommended must read. My recipes are based on his incredible research and analysis. I am so thankful for Gabriel's dedication to promoting the best Raw principles in a medical, scientific and spiritual manner that is fun and easy to read. Cousens explains how miso can help us avoid certain kinds of radiation problems. I notice that tons of people now use cell phones. The reality is that these cell phones give off a certain amount of radiation, even when not in use. Eating miso may help to alleviate and prevent certain health risks associated with radiation.

Miso is the only non Raw ingredient in this book; it is considered a Living food because of its active live enzymes. It has no cholesterol, is low fat, contains isoflavones and is gluten free. I love the flavor that miso imparts, the depth and energy it adds to the recipes. You can find it at most health food stores as well as Whole Foods and online. Miso Master makes a high quality organic product that I recommend.

SEA SALT: There are different varieties and brands in the stores. Try to find sea salt rather than regular table salt.

COCONUT NECTAR: This is a new all natural sweetener that I really love and often recommend. You can make your own sweetener by blending some raisins or pitted dates with some water, but coconut nectar is already packaged and ready to use. It actually has no sugar, is very low on the glycemic index, has living enzymes, is neutral Ph and very good to use in my recipes. You can buy it from Whole Foods Market, health food stores or online. I predict that this will be the next major food trend and popular sweetener! I enjoy the flavor and can feel the health benefits when I use it in my recipes.

FRESH YOUNG THAI COCONUT: We will use these often in recipes. Young fresh coconuts from Thailand are good and can be found at your local health food store, Asian store or Whole Foods Market. Please as them to open them up for you, that is the best, easiest and safest way. They should open the coconut for you if you ask, but if they won't or can't and you must open it yourself, please be very careful!

IMPORTANT: For the safest technique, PLEASE place the coconut on a sturdy table or surface that can withstand a lot of pressure. With a large, heavy, sharp knife, a butcher knife being the best, hold the handle firmly and make strong, firm chops on the top of the coconut, forming a square in order to open the top. NEVER put your hand near the coconut when chopping it! Make sure no one is within a 10 foot radius. You are chopping with a very sharp knife in your hand, and pieces of coconut will fly around. I have seen people hold the coconut while trying to chop it open and have heard too many stories of people cutting themselves. Please be safe.

To continue, the best way to open a coconut is to chop a square "lid" on top. After each chop, put the knife down and turn the coconut to make another chop at a 90 degree angle to the previous cut, so that eventually you have a square lid that you can lift and get to the coconut water and flesh.

In recipes that call for coconut water, pour the water into a bowl and strain out the coconut fiber and particles before adding it to your recipe. If the recipe does not call for coconut water but for coconut flesh, you can drink the water or put it in a glass jar and store in the refrigerator to use later. Use a large spoon to scrape out the coconut flesh or meat, and also carefully scrape or remove all debris, coconut splinters and fiber from the coconut flesh and meat before using in the recipe. You want to get all of the fibers out, as they do not blend, taste, or digest well. Please make sure that no splinters, fibers or hard pieces of coconut shell make it into your blender. In some recipes, if you do not have access or can't find any fresh young coconuts, you may substitute almond milk…or grow your own coconut palm trees!

ORGANIC GOJI BERRIES: These have not caught on in America yet, but I am doing my part to promote them as one of the best all natural healthy superfoods or snacks you can eat! They are sundried, so have absorbed super energy, plus they have built in super nutrition. There are many websites to promote them. Some of their amazing health benefits: They have the highest amount of antioxidants, they have 500 times more vitamin C per ounce than oranges, and they have super amounts of vitamins A, B1, B2, B6 and E. They have more beta carotene than carrots, and in certain studies have been found to have anti-aging and anti-cancer properties.

ORGANIC EXTRA VIRGIN COCONUT OIL: I love coconut oil in many of my desserts. It is like an all natural pastry cream! But with tons of good, natural, high quality fat, it has no cholesterol in its raw form and is not a trans fat. You can put it in your hair for extra shine. Eating it will bring out natural beauty from within and it tastes amazingly great!

RAW STAR RECIPES

ORGANIC GOLDEN FLAX SEEDS: These are versatile, healthy and fun to eat. It is easier to buy them pre-ground: http://www.FlaxUsa.com. When you blend or grind them yourself in the blender, you are exposing them to heat. They start to oxidize and break down quickly, losing nutrients. FlaxUSA has a special slow cold milled process that locks in valuable nutrients, vitamins and minerals. The flax seeds are not exposed to heat, so they last up to 22 months in the container, and their prices are amazing. FlaxUSA is the #1 flax farmer and company in the USA, so I like to recommend and use their products.

Other ingredients that I use, such as Organic zucchini, limes, carob powder, etc., are pretty common and easy to find. Make sure they are all Raw and Organic. Just to be sure, once again, that ALL ingredients in the recipes are RAW & ORGANIC.

KITCHEN SAFETY: I want to remind everyone to be safe and aware and to exercise common sense. When cutting or slicing with a knife, curl your holding fingers so they don't get cut. If you drop a knife, take a step back and never try to catch it. Always wear closed toed shoes to protect your feet and to keep from slipping. No slippers or going barefoot in the kitchen or prep areas, please.

Although these recipes are fun and safe for children to make, parents please make sure the kids are ALWAYS supervised! And kids, please do not make these recipes by yourself. Please always have an adult help you or be with you when making these recipes!

NEVER put your hand into the blender, even if you think it is unplugged or turned off. It is always better to be safe than sorry, and this is especially true in the kitchen. If you are not careful or you fool around, you can cause serious harm or severe injuries that may not be fixed. The kitchen is a fun and creative place, but please use caution and common sense to get the maximum enjoyment from your experiences.

With all of that said, let's get started and have some fun!

Spinach Herb Dip

A rich, smooth dip for all of your raw organic veggies and snacks. Use as a spread or even put a little on top of a soup for garnish. It adds a nice creamy touch to your favorite foods.

THEME: INDIAN | SERVINGS: 2–3

INGREDIENTS

2 Cups Raw Organic Baby Spinach Leaves

1 Organic Avocado

1 Cup Organic Cilantro or Parsley or a combination of both

Finely chopped Organic Basil and Rosemary

1 Tablespoon Organic Curry Powder or Turmeric

1 Tablespoon Organic Miso Master Chickpea Miso

1 Tablespoon Tahini

Sea Salt to taste

1/4 Cup Water

DIRECTIONS:

Pour the water first into the blender, then seed the avocado, being careful to take out the little stem part on top, and scoop it in; add all the other ingredients and blend until smooth.

Serve with raw organic greens and white asparagus tips, on heirloom tomatoes, purple cabbage leaves cut into triangle shapes, sliced radishes, fresh pea pods and yes, even carrot and celery sticks.

Spinach and other raw organic greens help to alkalize the body's Ph. The more neutral to positive Ph your body is, the healthier and more optimal it becomes. Balanced and well researched raw organic gourmet recipes help you to accomplish this naturally, with the most enjoyable dining experiences ever! Each bite becomes a celebration and adventure into "superfoods."

Curried Hummus

People often ask, "Where do you get the protein?" In addition to nuts, avocados and olives, which are all high quality proteins and fats, chickpeas also provide a great source of protein, especially when they are sprouted and soaked overnight or for a few days. Always rinse with fresh clean water, keep covered in a cool dry area, and do a final rinse and drain before using.

THEME: INDIAN | SERVINGS: 2–3

INGREDIENTS

2 Cups Raw Organic Baby Spinach Leaves

1 Organic Avocado

1 Cup Organic Cilantro or Parsley or a combination of both

Finely chopped Organic Basil and Rosemary

1 Tablespoon Organic Curry Powder or Turmeric

1 Tablespoon Organic Miso Master Chickpea Miso

1 Tablespoon Tahini

Sea Salt to taste

¼ Cup Water

DIRECTIONS:

Pour the water into the blender first, then add the rest of the ingredients in and blend until smooth.

Pita or Lettuce Wraps: Using red lettuce leaves, chard leaves or romaine lettuce, spread the curry hummus down the middle of each leaf. Add sliced avocado, sliced olives, chopped tomatoes, cubed cucumbers, sunflower sprouts, drizzle with olive oil and enjoy!

Variations: You can try the Pine Nut Sauce from the Falafel Recipe.

You can also use sundried nori wraps (sushi seaweed sheets is the common name). Find the sundried variety with all the enzymes and nutrients intact, as most are toasted or roasted. The Eden brand has one of the best organic sushi seaweed sheets from protected oceans. You can roll the curry hummus in them for a quick snack; some people even use the sushi wrap and add lettuce leaves, either outside or inside, then roll them to make a quick fresh wrap. You can call it a curry sushi wrap! You can also use the Spinach Dip in place of the curry hummus, too. Get creative and have fun!

RAW STAR RECIPES

Nuggets

Everyone loves dipping nuggets into a nice BBQ sauce. One of my surfer friends calls good waves in Hawaii "Nuggets", his way of describing something really good. That is a good description of this party favorite.

THEME: AMERICAN | SERVINGS: 3–4

INGREDIENTS

1 Cup Ground Raw Organic Golden Flax Seeds

1 Tablespoon Raw Organic Tahini

3 to 4 Tablespoons of Organic Miso Master's Chickpea Miso

Chopped Rosemary and Basil (both are optional or add your favorite fresh herbs)

5 Tablespoons Olive Oil

2 Tablespoons Water

Sea Salt to taste

Maine Coast Sea Vegetables Company's Kelp Granules with Cayenne Pepper

Finely Chopped Basil

DIRECTIONS:

Grind the Raw Organic Golden Flax Seeds in the blender until they become a fine powder, or use pre-ground organic flax seeds from Flax USA.

Mix with all the other ingredients in a large bowl. Kids and adults love to help make this recipe. You can make all sorts of fun shapes with your hands or with cookie cutters.

If you grind the flax seeds yourself, they are exposed to high temperatures, start to oxidize, and are hard to clean and store. Flax USA's pre-ground seeds are convenient, with nutrients locked in up to 22 months through their low-temp cold-milled technique. Flax USA makes it fun and easy!

Please use any of the dips, sauces or dressings in this book to compliment this dish.

Avocado & Grapefruit Salad with Pickled Radish

Many high-end spas and resorts around the world serve a refreshing fruit salad. This is a gourmet version and twist on a classic recipe.

THEME: AMERICAN | SERVINGS: 2

INGREDIENTS

1 Organic Avocado

1 Organic Radish

1 Organic Grapefruit

1/3 Cup Raw Organic Bragg's Apple Cider Vinegar

2 to 3 Tablespoons of Coconut Nectar

A green leafy garnish of your choice (photo shows Organic Dandelion)

Organic Yellow round mini Zucchini (optional)

DIRECTIONS:

Prepare the avocado and plant the seed (grow an avocado tree!); peel and skin the grapefruit and cut into slices. Quarter the avocado and place on edge to form a circle (see photo) in the center of your plate. Place the grapefruit slices to form a circle on top of the avocado. Using the RAW STAR Ceramic Peeler or RAW STAR Ceramic Knife, carefully cut very thin slices of radish and yellow zucchini (optional).

Cut very thin "noodles" or "toothpicks" from thin slices of radish and put in a bowl with a mix of Apple Cider Vinegar and Coconut Nectar. Let this sit for a few minutes to "pickle" the radish. After a few moments, place the thinly sliced radish on top of the grapefruit, arranging the other slices around the plate to decorate it, or place atop thinly sliced yellow zucchini (see photo). Put your favorite green leaf in the very middle as garnish and serve.

Variations: As a substitute for the coconut nectar, you can make your own sweetener with some water and raisins or dates blended in a blender and adjusted to your liking. However, new coconut nectar is very healthy, with no sugar, a low glycemic index and neutral Ph, and living enzymes. You will feel amazingly healthy after just trying it once!

RAW STAR RECIPES

Garlic Potato Chips

Tastes surprisingly "deep fried," very crunchy, tasty and satisfying. Definitely worth the effort and time! This recipe requires a dehydrator; the Good4U Brand is my favorite and recommendation for performance, quality and price.

THEME: AMERICAN | SERVINGS: 4–5

INGREDIENTS

1 Organic Golden Potato

1 Organic Garlic

1 Organic Lime, juiced

Sea Salt (optional)

1/3 Cup Organic Olive Oil (optional)

DIRECTIONS:

In this situation, using my RAW STAR brand of ceramic peeler or knife actually keeps the potato fresher longer, protects the flavor and keeps it pure in a way that metal or stainless steel cannot.

Peel the Organic Golden Potato into slices or use the RAW STAR Ceramic Knife to carefully make very thin potato slices. Dip each slice into the lime juice in a bowl, making sure both sides are well coated, then dip it into a second bowl with the olive oil, again ensuring that both sides are well coated. (Use the olive oil if you want a more deep-fried look and taste, but you do not have to use olive oil if you want a dry potato chip.) Lay the slices on the dehydrator tray and sprinkle very finely chopped organic garlic on top. You can sprinkle a little sea salt on top at this point as well.

Dehydrate at the highest temperature at first, then after 10 minutes slowly turn down the temperature to 114° in the Good4U Dehydrator. Set the timer for 6 to 8 hours. You want to flip them over one time, halfway through the dehydration process, so in 3 to 4 hours flip all the chips to the other side so both sides are properly dehydrated. The garlic stays on.

Put the leftover chips into a air tight glass jar and they will last a up to a month or longer.

People complain that dehydrated potatoes have a starchy taste, but I discovered that dipping the slices into the lime juice and adding garlic somehow gets rid of any starchy consistency or taste, and the chips come out perfectly RAWmazingly RAWlicious!

Kale Chips

Tastes surprisingly "deep fried" like a potato chip, but this is green, healthy and actually good for you! A great way to get more greens into your diet. Very crunchy, tasty and satisfying. Definitely worth the effort and time! This recipe requires a dehydrator.

THEME: AMERICAN | SERVINGS: 4–5

INGREDIENTS

1 Bunch of Organic Dino Kale (you can use other kinds of Organic Kale as well)

1/4 Cup of Organic Olive Oil

Sea Salt (Optional)

DIRECTIONS:

Wash and clean the dino kale properly. You can use other types of kale, but dino kale makes the best "chips." Simply coat both sides with olive oil by dipping it into oil on a plate or using your fingers, then sprinkle a little sea salt and place on the trays in the Good4U Dehydrator, at the highest temperature first, then in the next 10 minutes slowly turn down the temperature to 114° and set the timer for 6 to 8 hours.

You can make these with or without the sea salt.

You can make these before you go to sleep, and when you wake up they are done and ready to eat!

RAW STAR RECIPES

Fruity "Tuna" Wraps

This is a favorite at many spas around the world. Everyone loves tuna with mayo because it is so creamy and a comfort food. Unfortunately, our oceans are polluted and mercury occurs naturally in the ocean as well as being an added pollutant by man. We can still enjoy the same creamy flavors and tastes, thanks to my unique Vegan "Tuna" recipe, which is even creamier than other versions and is more healthy for you, too. It does not come from a can and has the high quality protein, fats and the benefits your body loves, so enjoy!

THEME: AMERICAN | SERVINGS: 4–5

INGREDIENTS

1 1/2 Cup Organic Cauliflower Tops

1/3 Cup Organic Walnuts

1 Lemon 1 or Lime, Juiced

1/4 Cup Water

2 Tablespoons of Miso Master Organic Chickpea Miso

Sea Salt to taste

Dash of Maine Coast Sea Vegetables Company's Kelp Granules with Cayenne Pepper

2 to 3 Tablespoons Organic Olive Oil to taste

2 Organic Pickles

DIRECTIONS:

Peel about 5 leaves from the napa cabbage or greens of your choice, and set on a plate. Cut a few grapes in half. Blend the rest of the ingredients, except for the pickles, in the blender until smooth, yet still retain a chunky consistency. Spoon the "tuna" mixture onto the cabbage leaves, and chop some pickles and put on top. You can add red bell peppers for color.

You will be surprised at how creamy and "tuna"-like this recipe is; refreshing, vegan, with no mercury or toxins at all. Aren't you glad you discovered Raw Organic Cuisine? It looks and tastes just like tuna fish with mayo!

Onion Rings

Tastes surprisingly "deep-fried," very crunchy, tasty and satisfying. A classic favorite that is definitely worth the time and effort. This recipe requires a dehydrator.

THEME: AMERICAN | SERVINGS: 4–5

INGREDIENTS

1 Large Organic Yellow Onion

1 Organic Orange (cut in half, use only 1/2 of the Orange)

1/3 Cup Organic White Sesame Seeds

1/4 Cup Water

1 Tablespoon of Organic Olive Oil

DIRECTIONS:

Using a good knife, slice the onion into desired thickness and pop out the rings. The thinner the rings, the faster they will dehydrate, but keep in mind that they will shrink somewhat in the Good4U Dehydrator. Place the sliced onion rings on a tray. In the blender pour in the water, then the sesame seeds and olive oil. Wash the orange carefully then cut it in half. Juice the half orange into the blender; chop the orange skin into small pieces and add to the mixture in the blender. The batter should be pretty thick; adjust the recipe until it is thick and batter-like.

Blend until very smooth and pour into a large mixing bowl. Simply dip the onion rings until well coated and place each well-coated ring on the Good4U trays. Turn it on at the highest temperature at first, then in the next 10 minutes slowly turn it down to 114° and set the timer for 6 to 8 or even 10 to 12 hours, depending on how crispy and crunchy you would like it to be. Make sure you do not over-dehydrate! Some people think that it will make it crunchier or crispier, but this is not true.

After making this recipe, you may want to play with it and adjust it to your liking by adding a dash of coconut nectar, less orange rind or less juice, etc. I encourage you to make it once, then decide how you want to adjust it, experimenting with flavors and crispiness.

These are very delicious, and look and taste like traditional deep-fried onion rings! Enjoy these with your lunch or as a snack. Store in an airtight glass jar for up to a month, or perhaps longer, depending on how long they have been dehydrated.

fresh

POP
CORN

DELICIOUS
NUTRITIOUS

RAW STAR RECIPES

Raw Organic "Buttered" Popcorn

This is so RAWmazingly refreshing and tastes so much like popcorn, but is actually hydrating, better tasting and good for you! It's also vegan, plant-based and healthy. People are totally RAWmazed at how much better it tastes than traditional popcorn, with that satisfying "buttery" taste and flavor and the nice crunch, too.

"Vegan" now is a trendy, hip, fashionable and healthy catchword, but you do not have to be vegan to enjoy vegan foods. It is good to balance out your diet and health with more plant-based foods, regardless of the type of foods you prefer. I hope that Eco Chef vegan recipes will change your mind about how delicious, fun, healthy, creamy and amazing vegan foods and recipes really are!

This recipe shows how "buttery" a vegan recipe can be. It will surprise you in healthy, fun ways. That is the point of Eco Chef recipes: good for you, good for the planet.

THEME: AMERICAN | SERVINGS: 5–6

INGREDIENTS

1/2 of an Organic Cauliflower

1/3 Cup Organic Olive Oil

3 to 4 Tablespoons of Organic Turmeric (adjust to taste)

Sea Salt to taste

DIRECTIONS:

In a medium bowl, whisk the olive oil and turmeric powder together until well blended by hand. This becomes the "butter" mixture.

Using your hands, break up the cauliflower into small popcorn-sized pieces. Mix into the "butter" mixture until well coated, sprinkle sea salt to taste, and serve.

"Fried Crab" Wonton

This is a fun Raw Organic recipe in keeping with the seafood-dominated Spa Cuisine served around the world. We are 100% Raw Organic Vegan in this recipe book, and part of the fun is coming up with the Raw Organic version of classic or traditional foods. In this recipe, finely sliced and chopped radish, mixed in either living hummus or brazil nut cheese, becomes the "Crab" filling. It looks and tastes very much like crab, with a slightly different flavor. Experiment; if you play with the recipe, you can get it very close to crab! Just add your favorite veggies, toppings and fixings.

THEME: AMERICAN | SERVINGS: 3–4

INGREDIENTS

3 to 4 Organic Radishes

A Few Organic Cherry Tomatoes

2 Organic Pickles

1 Organic Yellow Beet or Yellow Bell Pepper or Orange Bell Pepper, cut into triangles

A few Organic Sprouts

1 Organic Lime, Juiced

A Pinch of Sea Salt, to taste

Raw Organic Living Hummus Recipe or Brazil Nut Cheese Recipe

DIRECTIONS:

Cut yellow radish or yellow bell pepper into square or triangle shapes. The "crab" mixture can be made in two ways, with finely chopped radish mixed with either Living Hummus or with Brazil Nut Cheese to give it a creamy "crab" consistency. To add more seafood flavor, use kelp with cayenne pepper and lime on top and a little sea salt.

Living Hummus is blended: 1/4 Cup Water, Sprouted Chickpeas, Tahini, Sea Salt, Olive Oil.

Brazil Nut or Pine Nut Cheese: 1/4 Cup Water, Olive Oil, Brazil Nuts or Pine Nuts, Chickpea Miso. (You can try lime or lemon juice rather than the miso). Blend until very smooth, then hand mix gently with cut red radishes and layer between the sliced yellow beets or bell peppers. Enjoy.

RAW STAR RECIPES

Stuffed Zucchini Flowers with Pineapple Salsa & Chili Oil

I love sharing this elegant example of what Raw Spa Cuisine is about: simple, refreshing, delicate, fantasy food that refreshes your soul and spirit. You have to get the zucchini flowers in season, and you can easily grow your own, too! The chili oil and chili pistachio nuts make this a true Eco Chef gourmet experience!

THEME: ITALIAN | SERVINGS: 4–5

INGREDIENTS

4 Organic Zucchini Flowers

1/2 Cup Organic Pineapple (from Hawaii is the best)

3 Organic Roma Tomatoes

1 Organic Mango (optional)

1 Organic Lime, juiced

Pinch of Cayenne Pepper

1/4 Cup Organic Olive Oil

Pinch of Sea Salt

Few Organic Pistachio Nuts

3 Tablespoons Coconut Nectar

DIRECTIONS:

Make sure the zucchini flowers are clean and place them on a plate. Chop and dice the pineapple, tomatoes and mango; place in a bowl and squeeze lime over the mixture, then sprinkle sea salt to taste. Mix with a fork, then gently insert the salsa into each zucchini flower.

In a separate bowl, mix the cayenne pepper into the olive oil, then and drizzle onto the zucchini flowers.

In a small bowl, toss the pistachios with a little coconut nectar and cayenne pepper. Place them on the plate, and serve. Do not eat the stems, only the flower part!

Yam "Chili Cheese Fries"

Tastes surprisingly "deep-fried" just like fries, very crunchy and satisfying. Worth the effort and time! In the photos I added "Chili Cheese" to make the yam fries even more satisfying and fun. This recipe uses a dehydrator.

THEME: AMERICAN | SERVINGS: 3–4

INGREDIENTS

1 Organic Yam

RAW ORGANIC VEGAN CHILI:

3 to 4 pieces of Sundried Organic Tomatoes, either soaked in water for 15 minutes or in a jar in olive oil (Or buy a jar of Raw Organic Olives and Sundried Tomatoes)

5 to 6 Organic Olives

Sprouted Black Beans (from the store)

Sprouted Lentils (from the store)

3 to 4 Tablespoons Organic Olive Oil

NACHO "CHEESE":

1/4 Cup of Water

1/3 Cup Pine or Brazil Nuts

3 to 4 Tablespoons of either Organic Turmeric or Curry Powder

2 to 3 Tablespoons Miso Master Chickpea Miso

3 Tablespoons Organic Olive Oil

DIRECTIONS:

Using my RAW STAR Ceramic Peeler (because it is the best peeler and will keep your food fresh and pure, making YOU the STAR in the kitchen), carefully peel the yam, then peel nice slices into shapes that you will enjoy. Some people like thin and some people like thicker shapes. You may also cut them into rectangular 'fry' shapes too, but is not necessary.

Simply place onto trays in the Good4U Dehydrator at the highest temperature, then in the next 10 minutes slowly turn down the temperature to 114° and set the timer for 6 to 8 hours. You can make these before you go to sleep, then when you wake up they are done and ready to eat!

Variations and options: Add sea salt or olive oil either when you place the strips on the tray or after they are done, but they are also perfectly delicious just the way they are, naturally. They come out so crispy, crunchy and are so much fun to make and eat. They last a few weeks in a airtight jar, but most people will finish eating them quickly!

To make the "chili," simply chop the soaked sundried tomatoes and put in a mixing bowl, chop the olives and add to the bowl, pour in the olive oil and mix well. (You can also find Raw Organic sundried tomatoes mixed with organic olives in your health food store or at Whole Foods Market to save time.)

Add the sprouted black beans and sprouted lentils from the health food store (Whole Foods Market carries them as well). Mix well by hand and you have instant Raw Organic Chili, like the photo. Use it to top the dehydrated Yam Fries.

To make the "Nacho Cheese," add the water first to the blender, then the pine or Brazil nuts, a few tablespoons of

either turmeric or curry powder, the miso and olive oil. Blend until smooth and pour over the "Chili" for the "Chili Cheese" Yam Fries. So creamy and simply delicious! Please use the photo as a guide.

You can soak and sprout your own lentils and beans in just a few days, in a covered bowl with pure water in a clean, dry area. Make sure you rinse the beans and lentils with fresh water each day for 1 to 2 days, and do a final rinse before using. Never use the soaking water, and don't soak them in the refrigerator, because cold temperature hinders the process of sprouting and the activation of the enzymes.

Hawaiian Pizza

America's #1 favorite food is the pizza! Here is a great Hawaiian version that will please all pizza fans. This Hawaiian Pizza is perfect for picnics, parties and large events. You can also use or add your favorite Raw Organic toppings.

THEME: HAWAIIAN & ITALIAN | SERVINGS: 2–3

INGREDIENTS

2 Chard Leaves

2 to 3 Roma Tomatoes

4 Sundried Tomatoes, soaked 10-30 minutes in water

1/4 Cup Olive Oil

1/4 Cup Water

Several Olives, sliced

Organic Hawaiian Pineapple

2 Tablespoons Chickpea Miso

Kelp Granules with Cayenne Pepper

Sea Salt to taste

Fresh Basil and Rosemary

Organic Sunflower Sprouts

Raw Organic Figs (optional)

QUICK PINE NUT "CHEESE"

1 Cup Pine Nuts

1/4 Cup Water

2 Tablespoons Olive Oil

PAN PIZZA "CRUST"

1 Cup Golden Flax Seeds

2 Tablespoons Water

2 Tablespoons of Olive Oil

Sea Salt to taste

DIRECTIONS:

In the blender, pour in the water first then add the sundried tomatoes, miso, olive oil, tomatoes, a few dashes of the kelp granules with cayenne, several pinches of sea salt and some finely chopped rosemary and basil. Blend to desired consistency, longer for a smooth sauce and shorter for a more chunky quality. Spread onto well-washed chard leaves.

Spin all the ingredients for the Quick Pine Nut "Mozzarella Cheese" in the blender.

Deep Dish Pan Pizza Crust: grind golden flax seeds in the blender until a fine powder. Put in a bowl and add water, olive oil and dash of salt to taste. Mix well and spoon half the mixture onto each plate to make two deep-dish pizza crusts. Using a fork, form a triangular pizza crust and pat it down so it stays together.

Pour the above tomato pizza sauce onto the crusts, add the pine nut "cheese" sauce and dress it with the toppings. You can drizzle more olive oil on top for that greasy pizza effect! You will need to use a fork to eat the slice of pizza, as the crust won't stay together if you try to pick it up with your hands.

Variations: For "ham," you can use Maine Coast Sea Vegetable brand dulse. If you cut it into certain shapes, it looks and tastes like "ham" or "bacon." You can use it to make a Raw BLT by placing the dulse between lettuce leaves, sprouts, tomatoes, and the above pine nut cheese sauce.

Makes 2 pizzas.

You can experiment with different "crusts" such as purple cabbage, lettuce or kale. Let your creativity and imagination shine.

This Hawaiian Pizza looks and tastes just like a baked greasy pizza; the best and most refreshing pizza in under 10 minutes! This is a pleasing gourmet favorite among my clients, family and friends.

The cayenne pepper helps increase digestion along with the enzymes in the pineapple. The figs add color and look like pepperoni or sausage. This is also a great way to get more greens such as chard, of which most people do not eat enough. This pizza creates a positive and alkalizing Ph that will keep you young and looking great.

"Pepperoni" Pizza

A plant-based, flourless, dairy-free, vegan, super-delicious "Pepperoni" Pizza that is amazing looking and tasting, this is a world's first and only recipe! You can only get it here, invented by Eco Chef Bryan Au for your enjoyment. I want people to change their minds about the words "vegan" and "healthy," because I have finally been able to combine the most healthy vegan foods with the look and taste of truly decadent "junk food" and comfort food with the same flavors, creamy textures and enjoyment. Now pizza is actually good for you and for the planet! This recipe requires a dehydrator. (You do not have to dehydrate the crust, but it does taste better if you do. The "pepperoni" requires a dehydrator.

THEME: ITALIAN
SERVINGS: 5–6

INGREDIENTS

PIZZA CRUST:

3/4 Cup Raw Organic Oats

4 Tablespoons Raw Organic Golden Flax Seeds, ground

6 Tablespoons Water

Pinch of Sea Salt

4 Tablespoons Organic Olive Oil

PIZZA SAUCE:

5 to 6 Tablespoons Organic Sundried Tomato and 4 Olives

2 Organic Roma Tomatoes

1 clove Garlic, chopped (optional)

"PEPPERONI":

4 Tablespoons Organic Sundried Tomato and 3 Olives, blended

Roma Tomatoes

1 clove Garlic, chopped

1 Tablespoon oRaw Organic Golden Flax Seeds, ground

1 to 2 Tablespoons Organic Olive Oil

"CHEESE":

1/3 Cup Raw Organic Pine Nuts (can use Brazil Nuts)

1/4 Cup Water

2 to 3 Tablespoons Miso Master Chickpea Miso

2 to 3 Tablespoons Organic Olive Oil

DIRECTIONS:

Using a fork, mix all pizza crust ingredients in a large mixing bowl until well blended. Form a large ball, then flatten into a pizza crust shape. You can use the crust as is and do not have to dehydrate it, but it is better if dehydrated, warm and with a better consistency. Experiment with the pizza crust in different proportions, with or without dehydrating.

Place crust in dehydrator at the highest temperature, then slowly turn down the temperature in the next 10 minutes to 114° and set the timer for 4 to 5 hours.

For the sauce, blend fresh tomatoes chopped with a little olive oil and water for a few seconds and place in a bowl. Chop the sundried tomatoes, either soaked in olive oil from a jar or soaked in water, into small pieces. Add to the roma tomato sauce, then mince garlic, chop green olives into tiny pieces, add your favorite Italian fresh herbs and spices and hand mix.

To save time, you can purchase premade organic sundried tomato and olive bruschetta topping in a jar from your local health food store. For the "pepperoni," add a few tablespooons of the sauce or the sundried tomatoes and olive topping to the blender along with a little olive oil, the chopped garlic and ground flax seeds (this helps to keep it together later). Blend for a few seconds and put into a mixing bowl.

Using a spoon and your hands, make tiny balls or scoops of this mixture, place on the Teflex dehydrator sheets, and flatten to form "pepperoni." You can also use a tiny round or circular cookie cutter to make perfect round "pepperoni." Sprinkling a little flax powder on top helps keep the "pepperoni" together. Dehydrate for 8 to 10 hours, flipping after 4 hours.

Blend all "cheese" ingredients until smooth and set aside in a mixing bowl. It is best to make this just before using.

After the crust has dehydrated for 4 to 5 hours, put the pizza sauce, "cheese" and "pepperoni" on top. You can serve it right away or dehydrate for another 30 minutes to warm it, then serve!

Calzone

This is similar to the Samosa recipe in this book but with a marinara, olive and nut cheese filling. I love calzones, and this one is sure to please. You can also add pineapple chunks to give it a Hawaiian flavor, or warm it in the sun for extra natural energy. Some people place a glass bowl over the top of the plate and place in the sun or in a sunny window, or use the dehydrator to "warm it up." All of the recipes are Raw and Organic to keep the nutrients, vitamins, enzymes and minerals intact for your maximum health benefits, flavor and enjoyment.

This is all new Raw Organic Cuisine at its best! Everyone loves to try new foods and recipes. Raw Organic food is good for you and for the planet, while being the easiest and most delicious cuisine possible. It will quickly become the next major food trend and media "diet," so share the good news and spread the word.

THEME: ITALIAN | SERVINGS: 2-3

INGREDIENTS

CALZONE "PASTRY":

2 Cups Raw Organic Golden Flax Seeds

1/4 Cup Water

2 Tablespoons Organic Olive Oil

Sea Salt to taste

MARINARA SAUCE:

1/2 Cup Roma Tomatoes

1/2 Cup Sundried Tomatoes

1/4 Cup Olive Oil

1 to 2 Olives

Sea Salt to taste

1 Tablespoon Miso Master Organic Chickpea Miso

Finely chopped Basil

NUT CHEESE:

1 Cup Brazil or Pine Nuts

1/4 Cup Water

1/4 Cup Olive Oil

2 Tablespoons Miso Master Organic Chickpea Miso

DIRECTIONS:

Blend flax seeds to a smooth, fine powder (or use a food processor). Pour into a medium bowl, add the water and sea salt, then mix with a fork so the mixture becomes a paste and is evenly moistened. Using your hands, pat the mixture into the bottom of the bowl. Add the filling ingredients into one half-side of the bowl because you will fold the other half over it to form a half moon calzone shape. I like to place some of the ingredients near the outer edge so they will show when you fold it and you can see the filling, for an artistic and appetizing presentation (see photo).

The Sauce: Blend the sundried tomatoes, after soaking in spring water for 15 to 20 minutes, (or use a jar of sundried tomatoes soaked in olive oil), miso paste, olive oil and Roma tomatoes. Add several pinches of sea salt, sprigs of chopped rosemary and basil (both optional), then blend to desired consistency, longer for a smooth sauce and shorter for a chunky quality.

The nut cheese: Blend all the ingredients. You can also use the "Nacho Cheese" Pine Nut Sauce from the Macaroni and Cheese recipe.

Pour the marinara sauce and some nut cheese over half the calzone pastry mixture, add sliced olives and pineapple (optional), and fold over to form a half-circle calzone. Use a fork to mark the edges (see photo).

Spanish Lasagna

Nothing can be faster or easier than this unique festive recipe, one of my most popular signature dishes. Many people new to Raw Organic Cuisine tell me this one tastes so "cooked" or "baked" that it amazes them, and are surprised when they find out how quick it is to prepare. I have had many people decide to go Raw after trying this wonderful, easy recipe. It is super creamy and delicious, too. Enjoy!

THEME: SPANISH & ITALIAN I SERVINGS: 4

INGREDIENTS

2 to 3 Avocados

2 Organic Zucchini

2 Organic Roma Tomatoes

4 to 5 Pieces Sundried Tomatoes, soaked for 10-30 minutes

1 Organic Lime

1/2 Organic Lemon

1/4 Cup Water

Maine Coast Sea Vegetables Company's Kelp Granules with Cayenne Pepper (optional)

Fresh Organic Basil and Rosemary

Sea Salt to taste

Yellow or Red Bell Peppers

2 to 3 Tablespoons Miso Master Chickpea Miso

Olive Oil

1 Cup Brazil Nuts

Few Organic Olives, sliced

DIRECTIONS:

What makes this recipe so special is how very quick and easy it is to prepare. It looks like it took you hours to make this gourmet entree, but it should only take 10 minutes! People love its creamy, festive textures and flavors.

First, use a vegetable mandolin to make thin slices of "pasta" with the zucchini, slicing them lengthwise. Marinate the slices on a plate with drizzled olive oil, lime juice and sea salt, then place in a 7" x 7" glass pan, making a thin layer across the bottom, slightly overlapping where the slices they meet.

Guacamole makes this dish creamy and Spanish! Seed the avocados, spoon into a bowl and mash with a few squeezes from the lemon. Add sea salt, miso, finely chopped rosemary, several dashes of kelp granules with cayenne, then add one chopped Roma tomato and sliced olives, mixing with a fork to desired guacamole consistency.

Spread guacamole on top of the zucchini layer in the glass pan. Squeeze a little more lime juice on top, and add chopped rosemary and kelp granules, then layer more thinly sliced marinated zucchini on top to form another thin layer.

Add water first to the blender, then the other Roma tomato, chopped basil and rosemary, the soaked sundried tomatoes, olive oil, sea salt and miso paste and blend until smooth. Pour and spread over the layer of thin zucchini in the glass pan.

Next, make "Ricotta Cheese" with the Brazil nuts! Add water first to the blender, then the nuts, a few squeezes of the lemon,

sea salt, finely chopped rosemary and 3 to 4 dashes of olive oil, and blend for 2 to 3 minutes.

Pour small amounts on top of the marinara sauce, resembling clumps of cheese (see photo). Add fresh, small, whole basil leaves, sprinkle more dulse granules and cayenne pepper on top, and you have the world's best and fastest Spanish Lasagna.

It is so creamy and delicious that I get a lot of requests for this one, and it is a huge favorite at my classes and lectures. It makes a great entree for a cafe or restaurant.

Pasta Alfredo

This one is also a favorite at RAW classes and restaurants alike. People are amazed at this quick, easy and delicious recipe, and it often motivates them to go further into Raw Organic. With a recipe so refreshingly delicious, it is easy to see why!

THEME: ITALIAN | SERVINGS: 2–3

INGREDIENTS

2 Organic Zucchini

1/4 Cup Olive Oil (adjust to taste)

Fresh Organic Rosemary and Basil (optional)

Sea Salt to taste

2 to 3 Tablespoons Miso Master Chickpea Miso

2 Cups Raw Organic Brazil or Pine Nuts

1/4 Cup Water

Lemon

1 Organic Roma Tomato

Organic Sliced Olives

DIRECTIONS:

Use a vegetable peeler or knife to create thin lengthwise slices of "pasta" from the zucchini, then use the knife to carefully cut "pasta noodles." Place on a plate, drizzle some olive oil on the "noodles," and hand mix to coat. This gives them the desired cooked look and taste.

For the "Alfredo Sauce": Add water, Brazil nuts, a few dashes of sea salt, miso, some finely chopped rosemary or basil (both optional) to the blender and blend until smooth. Adjust the water and olive oil to create the desired consistency.

Pour the sauce over the zucchini noodles, toss with chopped Roma tomatoes, olives and other favorite vegetables with a dash of olive oil and sea salt, top with chopped fresh basil and rosemary, and enjoy!

Angel Hair "Pasta"

This Angel Hair Pasta is quick and colorful. The yams make up the Angel Hair "Pasta" and literally give off a vibrant glow. The decadently velvety sauce plays well off the flavor of the yams. A surprisingly delicious and refreshing recipe. Yams are a favorite natural anti-aging food and a "health secret" among super models and celebrities.

THEME: ITALIAN | SERVINGS: 2–3

INGREDIENTS

1 Large Organic Yam or 1 Butternut Squash

1 Cup Raw Organic Brazil or Pine Nuts

Fresh Basil (optional for a Pesto Sauce)

1/4 Cup Olive Oil

2 to 3 Tablespoons Miso Master Chickpea Miso

Sea Salt to taste

1/4 Cup Water

Raw Organic Diced Tomatoes and sliced Olives for garnish

DIRECTIONS:

This is a really quick and tasty meal and it looks quite gourmet as well. Peel the yams with the RAW STAR Ceramic Peeler, then make strips using a fine grater. (You can use the RAW STAR Ceramic Peeler to make slices, then cut the noodles by hand with a knife also). Carefully place the angel hair yam "pasta" onto a plate, drizzle with olive oil and squeeze lemon juice on top to marinate.

Make a Pesto or Alfredo Sauce for the topping. In blender, first pour the water then add nuts, olive oil, sea salt and miso, blending until smooth and adding basil if you would like Pesto Sauce.

Pour the sauce over the Angel Hair Yam Pasta, add the diced tomatoes and sliced olives, sprinkle the dulse granules and cayenne pepper on top, and serve this very colorful, festive entree, made in just a few minutes.

Variations: You can also try other sauces such as the marinara sauce, or create a Hawaiian pineapple miso sauce. Use your creativity and imagination!

Pasta Marinara: You can also substitute the yams with grated zucchini or butternut squash and add the Marinara from the Hawaiian Pizza recipe. Add "meatballs" by using the "Ground Beef" recipe from the Taco recipe, using your hands to roll "meatballs."

"Sushi"

These quick, fun "Sushi" Rolls are Vegan and will totally amaze your friends. Rather than nori or seaweed, I use thinly sliced yam or zucchini for that unexpected new twist and flavor. These California Rolls and "Sushi" are refreshing and tasty, have an artistic, gourmet look, and are a crowd pleaser. I invited some friends over for a California "Sushi" Roll Party and we spend the whole time making "Sushi" and Dim Sum with leftover vegetable pieces, and it was so much fun!

THEME: JAPANESE | SERVINGS: 3–4

INGREDIENTS

2 Large Organic Zucchini or 2 Yams

Organic Purple Cabbage Leaves

A few Organic Pineapple pieces from Hawaii

2 Organic Haas Avocados

A few Tablespoons Miso Master Organic Chickpea Miso

1 Organic Papaya from Hawaii

Some Organic Sunflower Sprouts

1 Organic Carrot

DIRECTIONS:

Using the RAW STAR Ceramic Peeler, carefully make thin lengthwise slices of both zucchini and yams and set aside. Cut the pineapple into small chunks. Scoop out large chunks of avocado and papaya and set aside. Place the pineapple, small slices of avocado and papaya (looks like salmon!) on one end of the zucchini slice and on one side of a yam slice. Put a little of your choice of miso atop the pile you just made, then put 1 to 2 sprigs of sunflower sprouts with their tops sticking out above the roll.

Carefully roll them into California Roll "sushi." You will find that the zucchini rolls easily and sticks together well. With the yam, you may need to use some carrot "string" to tie it together so it does not unravel after you roll it. You may also use this for the zucchini rolls, for color and presentation.

Now you can alternate different ingredients in the rolls for different color and taste combinations. When you are done you will have bits and pieces of zucchini, yam, purple cabbage and carrots left over. Don't throw them away or compost them just yet! Use them to make hors d'oeuvres, dim sum or finger foods by cutting the cabbage and the various pieces of vegetables and fruit you have into interesting slivers and shapes. A dab of miso, pineapple, various pieces and slivers of vegetables make great-looking and tasting finger food. Assemble them to form interesting edible art!

The miso has a nice salty soybean flavor, but if you would like dipping sauce you can combine some azuki bean miso with a little water or blend some pineapple with a little mellow miso, sea salt and water to make a dozen or more servings. You may also try the different dressings for dipping sauces too.

"Macaroni & Cheese"

A RAW Vegan Organic Macaroni & Cheese recipe that is all natural and dairy-free, yet is creamy and amazingly delicious! I came up with a fun Raw Organic version out of necessity, as the cooked version was my favorite as a kid until I found out about the artificial colors, chemicals and preservatives that went into it! Some day things like that will be a distant memory. That is what is exciting about RAW Organic Cuisine; it is pure, healthy and deliciously all natural.

I brought this to a Thanksgiving potluck and it disappeared in an instant! It is a great holiday dish, with inviting presentation and colors. I hope you enjoy this special creation of mine as a popular comfort food. I want to bring out more new, innovative, never-before-seen Raw Organic Recipes and foods. My version of mac and cheese looks and tastes cooked and is the creamiest!

THEME: AMERICAN | SERVINGS: 5

INGREDIENTS

2 Large Organic Peeled Yams

Few Tablespoons Organic Olive Oil

1 Organic Lemon (optional)

"NACHO CHEESE" SAUCE:

1/3 Cup Raw Organic Brazil or Pine Nuts

2 Tablespoons Organic Turmeric

1/4 Cup Olive Oil

1/3 Cup Water

2 Tablespoons Miso Master Chickpea Miso for less salty flavor, 3–4 Tablespoons for stronger flavor

DIRECTIONS:

Using the RAW STAR Ceramic Peeler, carefully make as many thin lengthwise slices of yams as you can, after peeling them first. Stack the slices of Yams on top of each other and carefully slice them into small, thin macaroni shapes with a knife.

Put "noodles" into a bowl or Pyrex glass pan, drizzle with olive oil and squeeze some lemon juice (optional) on top. Mix the yams, making sure all the pieces are covered in olive oil, then set aside to allow them to marinate.

Combine all ingredients for the "Nacho Cheese" Sauce in a blender, blend until smooth, pour on top of the yams and mix again until all the pieces are covered in the "cheese" sauce. Let sit for 10 minutes to absorb the sauce and soften, then enjoy!

Please cover and refrigerate any leftovers.

Tacos

I have created a very interesting "ground beef" made from blended raw organic sunflower seeds and olive spread or tapenade that you can buy in a jar, or blend your own with pitted olives, olive oil, a tiny bit of sea salt and lemon juice, and you have greasy "ground beef." This will be used in the Tacos, Super Nachos, Tostada and Burritos. Taco fans rejoice, as this new RAWmazing version will be a real fiesta!

THEME: MEXICAN | SERVINGS: 2–3

INGREDIENTS

4 Pieces Organic Lettuce

1/2 Cup Raw Organic Sunflower Seeds

2 to 3 Tablespoons Kalamata Olive Spread from a Jar or Tapenade

2 to 3 Tablespoons Organic Olive Oil

1 Organic Lime

Sea Salt to taste

2 Organic Diced Tomatoes

2 Tablespoons Miso Master Organic Chickpea Miso

2 Large Organic Avocados

Maine Coast Sea Vegetables Company's Kelp Granules with Cayenne Pepper

Few Sliced Organic Olives

Organic Sunflower Sprouts

1 Red Organic Bell Pepper

DIRECTIONS:

"Ground Beef ": Blend sunflower seeds to a semi-smooth consistency that is still chunky, around 2 minutes. You want it to be the same consistency as ground "you know what!" Put in a bowl and add the olive spread, olive oil, sea salt and a few drops of lemon. Mix with a fork and fluff it up, and it should start to look like ground "beef." Set aside. This can be used to make "meatballs" for the marinara pasta recipe, or for hors d'oeuvres and finger foods.

Guacamole: Scoop out the avocados and put into a bowl, adding sliced olives, diced tomatoes, miso, a few dashes of sea salt, 2 to 3 large squeezes of lime and a sprinkle of dulse and cayenne pepper, then mash with a fork to desired consistency.

Seed the red bell pepper and blend until it forms a thick paste. Set aside to add to the tacos right before serving.

Fill the folds of lettuce with the "ground beef" mixture, add the guacamole, some diced tomatoes, sliced olives, top with the sunflower sprouts, drizzle with the red bell sauce and enjoy!

Variations: Use "Nacho Cheese" Pine Nut Sauce for the cheese flavor, and grated carrots or slivered yellow string beans for the cheddar cheese look.

Make pineapple salsa by mixing chopped pineapple with tomato chunks, cilantro and sea salt. Try chard leaves or different types of lettuce for the taco shell.

Burrito: use small chard leaves and wrap the above mixes in desired portions into a burrito. These are perfect on the beach, at a picnic or fiesta.

Super Nachos

Everyone loves Nachos, and now there is a super Raw Organic Living version to try! Kids love the fluorescent colors of this recipe. It is bright and festive, perfect for parties and to start off any Mexican meal.

THEME: MEXICAN | SERVINGS: 2–3

INGREDIENTS

2 to 3 large Purple Cabbage Leaves

Pea Pods (optional)

Guacamole

Diced Tomatoes

Sliced Olives

"Nacho Cheese" Pine Nut Sauce

Lemon or Lime Sea Salt

"GROUND BEEF "

Sunfower Seeds

Olive Spread

Sea Salt to taste

Lemon

DIRECTIONS:

Cut purple cabbage leaves into triangular nacho chip shapes and layer them on a plate. You can also use pea pods for the chips.

Add finely grated yams, guacamole from the Spanish Lasagna recipe, "Nacho Cheese" Pine Nut Sauce from the Tamale recipe, sliced olives, diced tomatoes, dulse granules with cayenne, lemon and lime juice and sea salt, sprinkle some "ground beek" mixture, and you have the world's most colorful, crunchy, super nachos!

Ground "Beef": Blend sunflower seeds to a rough "beefy" consistency, and mix with olive spread, sea salt and lemon juice to taste in a bowl for instant, Raw, Organic Vegan "ground beef."

Pad Thai

This recipe demonstrates how Raw Organic Food can easily look and taste cooked. This is one of my most popular recipes; people just can't seem to get enough of this one. It is a good one to have on hand to share with guests; it can be made ahead of time and lasts for several days in the refrigerator if you keep the sauce separate. The Almond Butter, Lime and Coconut Nectar Sauce really makes this RAWmazing and RAWlicious! One of the most popular Raw Organic Cuisine dishes to impress your family and friends, and so easy to make, too!

THEME: THAI | SERVINGS: 2–3

INGREDIENTS

1 Large Organic Yam

2 Large Organic Zucchini, one yellow and one green if possible

1 Cup Organic Mung Bean Sprouts

2 Organic Kale Leaves

2 Purple Organic Cabbage

Bunch of Organic Basil & Rosemary

1 Organic Lime, juiced

Maine Coast Sea Vegetables Company's Kelp Granules with Cayenne Pepper

1/4 Cup Organic Olive Oil

2 to 3 Tablespoons Miso Master Organic Chickpea Miso

A few Raw Organic Brazil Nuts, Almonds or Pine Nuts, finely chopped into thin slices

1 to 2 Tablespoons Coconut Nectar

3 to 4 Tablespoons Raw Organic Almond Butter

1 to 2 Teaspoons of Raw Organic White Sesame Seeds

DIRECTIONS:

Using the RAW STAR Ceramic Peeler, make thin lengthwise slices of yam and zucchini. Using a knife, carefully cut the slices into long, thin "noodles." Cut the kale and purple cabbage leaves in the same way, into long strips. Add the mung beans, gently mix all of the above in a large bowl and set aside.

In a separate bowl, mix the olive oil, dulse and cayenne pepper and some of the lime juice together (saving some lime juice for the sauce), then pour on top of the "noodles." Mix and serve with chopped pine nuts, basil and rosemary on top.

To make the Thai Sauce, mix almond butter with lime juice and coconut nectar to taste to make a really delicious new Thai Sauce. Squeeze more lime juice on top of entire dish as well. Sprinkle the sesame seeds on top and serve.

This is an exotic, colorful dish. Add some fresh chili peppers to make it spicy!

Note: You can make your own sweetener by blending a bit of water with raisins or pitted dates, or substitute 2-3 tablespoons of coconut nectar.

"Beef Stir Fry" with Teriyaki Sauce

This all new recipe is similar to the fake tofu meats that you can enjoy in vegetarian or vegan restaurants. The "beef" here is Organic eggplant and you can easily make it fresh at home and impress your friends! It is simple, very tasty, and actually looks and tastes like "Beef Stir Fry." You need a dehydrator for this recipe. (If you over-dehydrate this recipe, it becomes a crispy, crunchy "Eggplant Jerky" that is delicious!)

THEME: CHINESE | SERVINGS: 2-3

INGREDIENTS

1 Large Organic Eggplant

1/3 Cup Organic Balsamic Vinegar

Dash Organic Olive Oil

Some Raw Organic White Sesame Seeds

1 Organic Red Bell Pepper

1 Organic head of Broccoli

1 Organic Red Onion

Your favorite herbs and spices or Maine Coast Sea Vegetable's Kelp and Cayenne Mix

TERIYAKI SAUCE:

1/3 Cup Coconut Nectar
(or make your own sweetener by blending water with raisins or pitted dates)

Dash of Organic Balsamic Vinegar mixed with Organic Olive Oil

DIRECTIONS:

Peel the eggplant, then make thin slices. Cut the slices into rectangular "beef strip" type of shapes, then use the knife to carefully score it, making crisscross lines on both sides to help it absorb the marinade and to give it a "beef" texture and look. (see photo)

In a medium bowl, mix the balsamic vinegar with olive oil and soak the eggplant pieces in this mixture. Add your favorite herbs and spices to give it more flavor. I use Maine Coast Sea Vegetable's brand of Kelp and Cayenne mix.

Place the eggplant strips in the dehydrator trays, dehydrating on the highest setting and temperature for the first 10 minutes, then slowly lowering the temperature in the next 10 minutes until you reach 114°. Set the timer to 12 hours, flipping the pieces over so both sides get properly dehydrated midway, at 6 hours. You want the eggplant to be slightly soft and not hard or crispy for this recipe. It should be ready at 12 hours, but may be done sooner.

After the "beef" eggplant pieces are done, put on a serving plate, chop and add the rest of the vegetables them. Combine sauce ingredients and hand mix or use blender to make the Teriyaki Sauce. Pour it over the "beef stir fry," sprinkle the sesame seeds, and serve.

Note: If you dehydrate the eggplant longer than 12 hours, it becomes crispy and crunchy Eggplant Jerky, which is a fun and delicious snack too!

RAW STAR RECIPES

"Steak"

This novel recipe actually looks and tastes like a steak, Raw Organic Living Cuisine now "meaty" and more fun! People often ask me for Raw Organic Living Cuisine versions of different food items; it is a challenge I enjoy. I finally came up with a "Steak" recipe, much to everyone's surprise and delight! You will find this recipe amusing and playfully delicious, another way to enjoy our favorite, tomato. Pair it with the Mashed Potato and Gravy recipe, a salad and favorite sliced vegetables on the side to have that "steak" dinner.

THEME: AMERICAN | SERVINGS: 2–3

INGREDIENTS

1 Large Organic Tomato

2 Tablespoons South River Brand Azuki Bean Miso or any Azuki Bean Miso

(Try Olive Tapenade rather than Miso, for a different flavor)

2 Tablespoons Organic Olive Oil

1 Organic Lime, juiced (optional)

DIRECTIONS:

Slice the tomato into inch thick slices, then cut into more square or rectangular steak-like shapes. In a bowl, mix the miso or tapenade, olive oil and lime juice together well, then cover all sides of the tomato slices with the azuki bean mixture, using a spoon or fork and shaping it steak-like. The texture of azuki beans gives it the look of a steak, while olive oil gives it the fried look and taste. When you cut into it, it even has that medium "rare" look!

This another fun way to eat a tomato, and when paired with traditional favorite side dishes is very satisfying, but this "steak" will help keep you young, fit and healthy! Being Raw Organic is about healing yourself and the planet. Increase your health while freeing up precious resources and allowing for real peace on Earth.

"Meat" Loaf

This is a lot like traditional meatloaf but is now vegan, plant-based and even better. I also invented a miso gravy that is super-nutritious and delicious. Living foods are comfort food!

THEME: AMERICAN | SERVINGS: 2–3

INGREDIENTS

2 Cups Raw Organic Sunflower Seeds

1/2 Cup Buckwheat Groats, soaked in water

3 Tablespoons Miso Master Organic Chickpea Miso

2 Cups Organic Golden Flax Seeds, ground (or Flax USA pre-ground)

1 Sprig Organic Rosemary, finely chopped

Maine Coast Sea Vegetables Company's Kelp Granules with Cayenne Pepper

1 Organic Lemon

Dash Sea Salt

1/4 Cup Organic Carrots, grated

2 to 3 Tablespoons Kalamata Olive Spread or Tapenade

1/4 Cup Water

GRAVY:

1 Cup Water

2 Tablespoons Azuki Bean Miso

4 Tablespoons Golden Flax Seeds, ground

DIRECTIONS:

Blend the golden flax seeds into a fine powder (or use a food processor, or pre-ground). Put into a bowl and set aside. To the blender add water, sunflower seeds, soaked buckwheat, miso, dulse and cayenne, lemon, rosemary and sea salt, and blend for 3 minutes. Pour into the flax seed mixture and make a large ball.

Knead until thick and shape into a loaf. Thinly cover the outside with the olive spread and garnish with basil.

Gravy: Add water to the blender, then miso and ground flax seeds, blending until smooth. Adjust consistency by adding more ground flax seed to thicken, or more water. It will start to thicken on its own after you make it, so you may want to add a bit more water and blend if it gets too thick…or just enjoy the thickness. Pour on top of the "Meat" Loaf just before serving.

You will have the best Raw Organic Vegan Gravy in the world, making the word *vegan* synonymous with desirable, gourmet and fashionable.

Variations: For an easier and cheaper Gravy, blend 1/4 cup water and 2 to 3 tablespoons of chickpea miso with 2 to 3 tablespoons of organic raisins, adding olive oil and sea salt to taste.

Mashed Potatoes & Gravy

This recipe doesn't actually use potato! Instead, we use cauliflower and pine nuts with olive oil to create the creamiest and most decadent "mashed potato" ever! You will totally love this new version.

THEME: AMERICAN | SERVINGS: 2–3

INGREDIENTS

MASHED "POTATOES":

2 Cups Raw Organic Pine Nuts (Can substitute Brazil Nuts)

1 Cup Organic Cauliflower Tops

Finely chopped Rosemary (optional)

1/4 Cup Organic Olive Oil

1/4 Cup Water

Sea Salt to taste

3 Tablespoons Miso Master Organic Chickpea Miso

GRAVY:

1 Cup Water

2 Tablespoons Azuki Bean Miso

4 Tablespoons Raw Organic Golden Flax Seeds, ground

DIRECTIONS:

Beginning with the water in the blender, add all the "mashed potato" ingredients and blend until smooth.

The Gravy: Blend the water, miso and flax seeds until smooth. Adjust consistency by adding golden flax seeds for thickness and water to make it thinner.

Pour on top of the "mashed potatoes" just before serving.

Vegetable Pie

A fun and easy vegetable pie that takes a few minutes to make. Very creamy, gourmet and amazingly easy!

THEME: AMERICAN
SERVINGS: 2–3

INGREDIENTS

Calzone / Samosa pastry mix

2 Cups Raw Organic Pine Nuts (Can substitute Brazil Nuts)

1 Cup Organic Cauliflower Tops

Finely chopped Rosemary (optional)

1/4 Cup Organic Olive Oil

1/4 Cup Water

Sea Salt to taste

3 Tablespoons Miso Master Organic Chickpea Miso

DIRECTIONS:

To make the vegetable pie, use the Samosa recipe for a flaky, delicious crust. Make two round balls with your hands, then flatten into two round circles. Carefully place one circle into a serving bowl and press down lightly.

Fill with the "Mashed Potato" recipe, blending all ingredients, then add chopped olives, tomato, fresh peas or your favorite vegetables. Gently put the second circle on top as the crust, and lovingly serve!

RAW STAR RECIPES

Sunburger with Fries

A new, fresh "Veggie Burger" with fries! Delicious and easy to make at home.

THEME: AMERICAN | SERVINGS: 2–3

INGREDIENTS

2 Cups Raw Organic Sunflower Seeds

1/2 Cup Organic Buckwheat Groats, soaked

3 Tablespoons Miso Master Organic Chickpea Miso

2 1/2 Cups Organic Golden Flax Seeds, ground (or pre-ground)

Dash of Maine Coast Sea Vegetables Company's Kelp Granules with Cayenne Pepper

Dash of Sea Salt

2 to 3 Tablespoons Kalamata Olive Spread

KETCHUP:

2 Organic Tomatoes, chopped

1/4 Cup Raw Organic Apple Cider Vinegar

1/4 Cup Organic Sundried Tomatoes, soaked

2 to 3 Tablespoons Coconut Nectar

GARNISH:

Organic Kosher Dill Pickles, Organic Sunflower Sprouts, Sliced Organic Tomatoes

FRIES & BUN:

2 Large Organic Rutabagas, sliced
1 Leaf Organic Lettuce

DIRECTIONS:

Blend the golden flax seeds into a fine powder (or use a food processor, or pre-ground). Put into a bowl and set aside.

Blend water first, adding sunflower seeds, soaked buckwheat, miso, kelp and cayenne, lemon and sea salt, and blend for 3 minutes. Mix in the flax seed and make a large ball. Knead until thick and then shape into a "burger." Thinly spread the olive spread around the outside and garnish with basil.

To make the fries: Thinly cut french fry-like pieces from the rutabaga. Sprinkle some kelp granules with cayenne and drizzle with olive oil to make spicy, "greasy" fries!

The Raw Ketchup: To the blender, add a little water with tomatoes, Bragg's vinegar, a dash of coconut nectar and sundried tomatoes, and blend until smooth. Serve as Ketchup.

Variations: To make a BBQ sauce, add pitted dates or raisins to this recipe, blend until smooth, and adjust seasonings to taste.

The Bun: You have choices! Thinly slice 2 pieces of rutabaga; use 2 lettuce leaves; or grind 1 cup golden flax seeds, mix with a few tablespoons water and olive oil and a dash of sea salt, then shape and compact into 2 "buns" with your hands. Depending on how well you mix or compact the flax seed buns, you might need to use a fork to eat it, or the bun may stay together well enough to pick it up with your hands. Try adding raw tahini and chickpea iso to make the "bun" stay together better.

Between the buns, first add a lettuce leaf, slice of tomato and the sun "burger," then garnish with pickles, sunflower sprouts, and ketchup. Add a side of rutabaga "fries." You can also slice yellow bell peppers into thin french "fries."

Most people are not aware that raw rutabaga has super health benefits: more nutrients than turnips and the most anti-cancer and cancer-fighting properties of the entire cabbage family, in which it belongs. To your health!

Sloppy Joes

Refreshing and fun "junk food" favorite! Get xloppy with Sloppy Joes!

THEME: AMERICAN | SERVINGS: 2

INGREDIENTS

2 Cups Raw Organic Sunflower Seeds

1 Tablespoon Kalamata Olive Spread or Tapenade

Organic Olive Oil to taste

1/2 Organic Lime, juiced

Sea Salt to taste

2 Organic Lettuce Leaves

MARINARA SAUCE:

1/2 Cup Organic Roma Tomatoes, chopped

1/2 Cup Organic Sundried Tomatoes, soaked in spring water 15 min.

1/4 Cup Organic Olive Oil

1/4 Cup Water

Few Organic Olives (optional)

Few pieces Hawaiian Organic Pineapple (optional)

2 to 3 Tablespoons Miso Master Organic Chickpea Miso

Maine Coast Sea Vegetables Company's Kelp Granules with Cayenne Pepper

Sea Salt to taste

Fresh Organic Basil and Rosemary, finely chopped (optional)

BUN RECIPE

from Sunburger

DIRECTIONS:

The Sauce: Blend the water, soaked sundried tomatoes, white miso paste, olive oil, chopped Roma tomatoes, a few dashes of kelp granules with cayenne and several pinches of sea salt with finely chopped rosemary and basil. Blend to desired consistency: longer for a smooth sauce and less time for a chunky quality.

The Patty: Add sunflower seeds and blend to a semi-smooth consistency that is still chunky. You want it to be a similar consistency as ground "you know what!" Put this in a bowl and add the olive spread from a jar, olive oil, sea salt and a few drops of lemon. Mix with a fork and fluff it up; it should start to look like ground "beef."

Add the marinara sauce to the "beef" bowl and mix. Spoon between 2 lettuce leaves, or between the Golden Flax Seed Buns from the Sunburger Recipe. The sliced olives and pineapple are optional twists. Use your creativity!

Chili Cheese Fries: Cut yellow bell peppers into long french

"fries" and pile them on a plate. Mix some azuki bean miso with the Sloppy Joe mixture and pour on top of the "fries"; drizzle some "Nacho Cheese" Pine Nut Sauce from the Macaroni & Cheese Recipe; and voila! Instant "Chili Cheese Fries." Add chopped tomatoes and drizzle a little olive oil on top for that "greasy" look and taste.

Burger Bun: Three choices, Thinly slice 2 pieces of rutabaga, use 2 lettuce leaves, or grind 1 cup golden flax seeds, mix with a few tablespoons water and olive oil, sprinkle a dash of sea salt, then shape and compact into 2 "buns" with your hands. Depending on how well you mix or compact the flax seed buns, you might need to use a fork to eat it, or the bun may stay together well enough to pick up with your hands. Also add raw tahini and chickpea miso to make the bun stay together better.

Variations: "Grilled Cheese"Sandwich

To make the bread, grind 1 cup of golden flax seeds to a fine powder in the blender or food processor, then mix in a bowl with 2 tablespoons of tahini and sea salt. Mix very well then use a fork to form a flat square on a plate; cut diagonally with a knife and separate the two halves. On one half, spread some "Nacho Cheese" Pine Nut Sauce from the Super Nacho Recipe. Use a spatula to carefully flip the other half on top to form a triangular "Grilled Cheese" Sandwich.

Open-Face "BLT" Sandwich

BLT fans can celebrate, because this is a good one! When you marinate the dulse in olive oil for a few minutes, it looks and tastes like "bacon" but without the sulfites, and it is actually good for you and the planet.

THEME: AMERICAN
SERVINGS: 2–3

INGREDIENTS

1 Cup Organic Golden Flax Seeds or Flax USA pre-grinded package

A few Tablespoons Raw Organic Tahini

Organic Olive Oil to taste

Sea Salt to taste

1 Organic Heirloom Tomato, preferably Pineapple variety

Maine Coast Sea Vegetables Company's Sundried Dulse marinated in olive oil

Organic Salad Greens, your favorite mix

DIRECTIONS:

Blend the golden flax seeds into a fine powder (or use food processor, or pre-ground), mix with tahini and a little olive oil and sea salt in a bowl, then roll into a ball with hands and press into a square shape like a piece of sandwich bread.

Place salad greens on top, a slice of heirloom tomato, and top with chunks or slices of dulse marinated in olive oil. Quick, easy, and thoroughly delicious!

Samosa

This Samosa looks and tastes like it is deep fried, but it is completely Raw Organic and an amazing superfood. You do not need to dehydrate it and can enjoy right after preparing it. Golden flax seeds can be hard to digest, but grinding them in this recipe allows easy assimilation; you get flavorful nutrition that is so simple to make.

THEME: INDIAN | SERVINGS: 2

INGREDIENTS

SAMOSA "PASTRY":

2 Cups Organic Golden Flax Seeds (or Flax USA pre-ground)

1/4 Cup Water

2 Tablespoons Organic Olive Oil

Sea Salt to taste

FILLING:

1 Organic Asian Pear, chopped into small cubes

2 Organic Figs, slicesd

Few Organic Cherry Tomato halves

Few Organic Kosher Dill Pickle Slices

Few Organic Fresh Peas

DIRECTIONS:

First, pour the flax seeds into the blender and grind to a smooth, fine powder (or use a food processor, or purchase Flax USA pre-ground). Pour into a medium bowl. Add water and sea salt, then mix with a fork so the mixture becomes a paste and is evenly moistened.

Using your hands, pat down the mixture into the bottom of the bowl. Add the filling ingredients into one half of the bowl, because you will fold the other half over to form a half moon-shaped Samosa! I like to place some of the ingredients near the outer edge so they will show when you fold it, for an artistic and appetizing presentation.

In this recipe, Asian pear substitutes for traditional potatoes and the figs give it a nice, sweet flavor as well as color. You can add bananas, turmeric or curry powder etc. to create your own delicious fillings.

Note: At the printing of this book, no one else has this recipe!

"Chicken & Turkey"

Part of the fun of being vegetarian and vegan is seeing what you can make that will taste like traditional meat dishes and comfort food to satisfying the emotions as well as the stomach. Here is a quick, easy and fun way to make "Chicken" or "Turkey" that you can use for entrees and for the holidays.

THEME: AMERICAN | SERVINGS: 3–4

INGREDIENTS

2 to 3 Fresh Young Coconuts, Meat carefully scraped

2 Tablespoons Organic Olive Oil

1/4 Cup Organic Turmeric

1/4 Cup Organic Curry Powder (optional)

A few Tablespoons Raw Organic Pine Nuts, chopped (optional)

A few Tablespoons Organic Ground Gold Flax Seeds

Sea Salt to taste

DIRECTIONS:

The Coconut: There are different techniques for scraping coconut meat. Be very careful and ensure that no one is around you when you are opening it.

To carefully get the creamy flesh out of the coconut, some people use a spoon and others like a rubber spatula, scooping out larger, chicken-like pieces. Carefully go over the coconut meat 2 or 3 times to make sure there are no splinters or shell pieces attached. These are hard to chew and don't digest well. Scrape all of the meat with a spoon to make doubly sure.

In general, there are 2 types of coconut flesh that you will encounter: thin, very soft, almost translucent, or thick and hard. (If it is purple, it is overripe and should be composted.) It may seem like a lot of work, but it gets easier with experience and is so worth it! Fresh, Raw Organic coconut is healthy, naturally anti-aging, with a special, unique flavor. For this recipe, you want to use the soft, almost translucent coconut flesh. Thicker, harder coconut flesh is best for desserts and smoothies, and can be stored in a glass container in the refrigerator.

The "Chicken": In a bowl or shallow pan, place the coconut flesh down, coat it with olive oil with your fingers, and sprinkle the turmeric, curry powder, sea salt, dulse and cayenne and olive oil over it. Sprinkle a little more turmeric and curry powder as needed. Mix it gently to make sure all the pieces are covered, let it sit for 10 minutes or longer, and serve. The longer you let it marinate, the more flavor it will absorb and the softer it will become.

For a "fried" or "baked" "Chicken," coat it with finely chopped pine nuts to make it extra crunchy, or use the flax seed powder to give it that "fried bread crumb" texture. Serve this with a side of salad, macaroni and "cheese" or "mashed potatoes" for a down-home comfort meal.

For "Turkey," marinate the coconut flesh in a mixture of: 1 cup of orange juice, 2 tablespoons chickpea miso and 2 tablespoons of coconut nectar first, then follow the "chicken " recipe. Feel free to experiment with different amounts of turmeric, curry powder, etc.

Variations: Add more spice and call it a Jamaican Jerk "Chicken" or Thai "Chicken." Use it at parties, pot lucks and holiday gatherings, or next to the Holiday Stuffing recipe!

Holiday Stuffing

This is a great Holiday Stuffing, perfect for Thanksgiving and other holidays. You can really give thanks to nature and all her splendor. The recipe is a delicious medley of fruit and veggies. A Raw Living Organic special treat!

THEME: AMERICAN | SERVINGS: 8

INGREDIENTS

2 Organic Asian Pears

1 Organic Mango peeled

1/2 Cup Raw Organic Golden Flax Seeds, ground

1/3 Cup Raw Organic Sunflower Seeds, soaked

Organic Butternut or Spaghetti Squash, few pieces, peeled and chopped

Organic Basil and Rosemary, finely chopped

Raw Organic Yams, finely grated (optional)

Large Organic Zucchini, grated

Few Organic Cherry Tomatoes, halved

1/3 Cup Raw Organic Pine or Brazil Nuts, chopped

5 Tablespoons Organic Olive Oil

3 Tablespoons Miso Master Organic Chickpea Miso

Sea Salt to taste

Organic Pomegranate

1/3 Cup Raw Organic Walnuts, chopped

DIRECTIONS:

Chop the pears and mangoes into small cubes, mix with the rest of the ingredients in a large bowl, top with pomegranate seeds and fresh hearbs, and serve!

The pomegranate adds a nice holiday twist and festive color.

Variations: Shape the Falafel Recipe into small cubes and add some "Ground Beef " from the Taco Recipe.

Now that you are eating living foods, you are connecting with the special forces and miracles in the universe, with health benefits that you have to experience to appreciate.

Raw Organic Living Cuisine always creates a cause to celebrate! I have been to many special holiday Raw Organic parties, events and potlucks. They are all very warm, loving, and super-creative. May you and yours enjoy all the health and joyful gifts in life.

Falafels

A Falafel recipe that does not require deep frying or dehydrating; one of my favorites and a good one to keep on hand in the refrigerator for parties or guess. It looks and tastes amazingly deep-fried! And it can be made fresh and quickly in just a few minutes.

THEME: MEDITERRANEAN | SERVINGS: 3–4

INGREDIENTS

1 Tablespoon Raw Organic Tahini

3 to 4 Tablespoons Miso Master Organic Chickpea Miso

1/2 Cup Raw Organic Chickpeas, soaked (optional)

Organic Rosemary and Basil, finely chopped

5 Tablespoons Organic Olive Oil

2 Tablespoons Water

Sea Salt to taste

"YOGURT" SAUCE:

1/2 Cup Raw Organic Brazil or Pine Nuts

1/4 Cup Water

2 Tablespoons Miso Master Organic Chickpea Miso

3 Tablespoons Organic Olive Oil

Organic Dill, finely chopped (optional)

Pinch of Sea Salt

1 Organic Lemon, juiced, to taste (optional)

Organic Golden Flax Seeds, ground (or FlaxUSA pre-ground)

DIRECTIONS:

Pour the water first into the blender (or food processor), then add all ingredients except for the tahini and flax seeds. Blend to a creamy, semi-chunky texture. Pour into a large bowl and hand mix the tahini and a few sprinkles of ground flax seeds, which help to keep the Falafel together.

Form small Falafel balls with your hands and put on a serving plate. Coat Falafel with more sprinkled flax seeds if you desire (optional).

To make the "Yogurt" Sauce: Pour the water into the blender first, then add all the ingredients except for the dill. Blend until creamy and smooth and pour on top of the Falafels. Garnish with some.

Serve with "Yogurt Sauce." Garnish with fresh chopped dill (optional) or your favorite organic greens, salads, tomato or cucumbers, and enjoy!

"Bacon & Eggs"

This is a fun, world's first, plant-based Vegan Raw Organic "Bacon and Eggs" recipe, another Eco Chef Bryan Au creation for your enjoyment. It is so easy, and it really looks like bacon and eggs! The "Bacon" recipe literally looks and tastes like bacon; the "Egg" is somewhat sweet, but will help lower your cholesterol rather than increase it. You saw it here first, folks!

Maine Coast Sea Vegetable Company is the only company I know that makes and packages their Organic Dulse Seaweed. This is a new ingredient for most people; it is quite salty, which you can cut by marinating in olive oil. Dulse seaweed contains many minerals, is sundried so the enzymes are active, has more fiber than oat bran, and is a great source of protein, iron, enzymes and vitamins A and Bs.

There are few new Vegan Raw Organic breakfast recipes out there, which is probably why my original Raw Organic Pancake recipe is so frequently copied. In response, I keep inventing new and original breakfast recipes. I am also inventing more raw organic recipes with no nuts, olive oil or dehydrating, but I will share new dehydrated ones too, just for fun.

THEME: AMERICAN | SERVINGS: 2–3

INGREDIENTS

1 Young Coconut

1 Organic Papaya (from Hawaii is best)

Dulse Seaweed (Maine Coast Sea Vegetables Company is the best)

Organic Olive Oil to taste

DIRECTIONS:

Carefully open up a young Coconut and scrape out the inside "meat" so that it comes out in one whole piece if possible. This will take practice! Using a knife, cut some oval "fried egg"-like shapes and carefully place on your plate (see photo).

Cut the papaya and carefully scoop out 2 round dome "Yolks." They are likely to be too large, so you can thinly slice them to make them flatter and more yolk-looking, then cut them into dome yolk shapes and place on top of the "egg," the young coconut meat on the plate.

On another plate, marinate some long dulse seaweed pieces lightly in olive oil for a few minutes to make them hard and crunchy like "bacon," and serve next to your "fried egg." It is best to eat the salty "bacon" first, then move on to the sweeter coconut and papaya "egg."

RAW STAR RECIPES

"Stir Fried" Asparagus Tips with Pineapple Salsa

This is a satisfying and easy raw organic recipe to make if you are in a hurry; people love it, so give it a try! It serves about 3 people. It works best if you can find really small "baby" asparagus, but is fine with larger stalks too. This recipe requires only simple chopping. Very refreshing and RAWlicious. Definitely a crowd and party pleaser.

When you use my RAW STAR Ceramic Knives, the food stays fresher, longer!

THEME: AMERICAN | SERVINGS: 3–4

INGREDIENTS

1 Bunch of Organic Asparagus

Few Organic Sundried Tomatoes in olive oil or soaked in water

1 Organic Pineapple (from Hawaii)

2 to 3 Organic Roma Tomatoes

1 Organic Orange or Red Bell Pepper

1/4 cup Organic Olive Oil

Dash of Kelp Granules and Cayenne Pepper

Pinch of Sea Salt

1 Organic Lime, juiced

DIRECTIONS:

Slice the asparagus into halves across the thicker part of the stems, to use only the tender tips.

Place on serving plate, drizzle with olive oil and sea salt, and let it marinate.

Finely dice and sliver fresh and sundried tomatoes, pineapple and bell pepper. Mix well in a bowl and squeeze some lime on top. Place the pineapple salsa on top of asparagus, sprinkle some dulse or kelp flakes with cayenne, and serve.

Pesto Kelp Noodles with Asparagus Tips

Kelp Noodles are all the rage in the Raw Organic Cuisine world at the moment. They are so quick and easy to use, you literally just open the package and rinse. This recipe with Pesto Sauce and Asparagus Tips is a high-end spa gourmet meal in an instant. Raspberries and basil are used as a colorful garnish in the photo, but you can use red cherry tomatoes cut in half as well and your favorite greens.

THEME: ITALIAN | SERVINGS: 3

INGREDIENTS

1 Package Kelp Noodles

1 Bunch Organic Asparagus

6 Fresh Organic Basil Leaves

1/2 Cup Organic Pine Nuts (nuts are optional)

1/2 Cup Organic Olive Oil Organic

Sea Salt to taste (optional)

Organic Raspberries as garnish (optional)

DIRECTIONS:

Open the kelp noodles, rinse in pure water, and put into a mixing bowl. Cut the asparagus into tip pieces and medium stalk sizes, and set aside in bowl.

Blend the basil leavess, pine nuts (optional, you don't have to use any nuts in this recipe) and olive oil until the basil is very small, like grains of sand. Pour the pesto over the kelp noodles in the bowl, add sea salt to taste (optional), mix well and put on a serving plate. Arrange with extra Asparagus tips on top and around as garnish. (You may add the asparagus tips while mixing the pesto sauce if you want it coated).

Variations: You may want to marinate the asparagus in olive oil, or cut them into slivers and marinate to give them a more "cooked" taste and presentation. You can try adding a small pinch of chickpea miso to the pesto sauce.

Garnish beautifully, serve and enjoy!

Spicy Schezuan Noodles

Be ready for a culinary adventure, this new recipe is spicy and tastes"stir fried"! We use the zucchini to make the "noodles." It is so much fun to make this; it only takes a few minutes and can satisfy your Asian Cuisine cravings or appetite.

THEME: CHINESE | SERVINGS: 2–3

INGREDIENTS

1 Organic Zucchini

2 Red Hot Chili Peppers, diced small

3 to 4 Tablespoons Organic Curry Powder

1/2 Organic Carrot, grated

1 Organic Baby Bok Choy with each leaf separated

Organic Broccoli Florets, chopped into small pieces

1 Yellow Organic Zucchini, thinly sliced (optional)

Sunflower sprouts (optional)

Organic Black Sesame Seeds

4 to 5 Tablespoons Organic Olive or Sesame Oil

Few string beans, julienned (optional)

Sea Salt to taste

Cayenne Pepper to taste (optional)

1/2 Organic Lime, juiced (optional)

DIRECTIONS:

At chef and kitchen stores they sell "spiralizers," or hand machines that make "noodles" from vegetables, varying in cost from $30 to $50. They are really fun to use, and make a lot of "noodles" quickly, in perfect shapes and sizes. The one used in this recipe (see photo) is from Sur La Table, a gourmet chef supply store with a great online store as well.

Peel the zucchini with the RAW STAR Ceramic Peeler. Using the hand machine, I made fine angel hair noodles from the zucchini.

Place the "noodles" in a large mixing bowl and add all the rest of the ingredients. Mix gently and well by hand until well coated, garnish and serve! Please use the photo as a guide.

Note: I recommend the RAW STAR Ceramic Peeler is because it will never rust and it protects the flavor of your food. Ceramic doesn't react or change the flavor of food like metal or stainless steel knives do, which is why gourmet chefs and kitchens now use ceramic cutlery. The RAW STAR line is the best quality at the best prices!

Tempura

Tastes "deep fried" and crunchy on the outside like tempura, but still soft inside. This recipe requires a dehydrator, and believe me, it is worth it!

The Good4U is my dehydrator of choice for its new design, high performance and great price. It comes with a digital timer. You can see through their trays to check on the food without opening it and letting out the heat, making it more efficient and fun to use than other dehydrators.

THEME: JAPANESE | SERVINGS: 4–5

INGREDIENTS

Your Choice of 1 Organic: Eggplant, Yam, Onion, Okra, String Bean, Kale

1 Organic Orange, cut in half

1/3 Cup Organic White Sesame Seeds

1/4 Cup Water

1 to 2 Tablespoons Olive Oil

DIRECTIONS:

This recipe follows the same process as the Onion Rings, using your favorite vegetables such as bell peppers, eggplant, green beans, or other typical tempura vegetables, and chopping them into small bite-sized pieces. Be sure to slice them very thin and small so that the vegetables will dehydrate all the way through and also makes the dehydration faster.

After chopping the vegetables, place them on a tray. Pour the water, in the blender, then add sesame seeds anda dash of olive oil. Wash the orange carefully, cut in half and juice into the blender. Chop the orange skin into small pieces and add to the blender. Blend until very smooth and pour into a large mixing bowl. The batter should be pretty thick in order to stick, so please adjust the recipe accordingly.

Dip the vegetables until well coated, then place each vegetable on the dehydrator tray. Turn it to the highest temperature setting, then in the next 10 minutes slowly turn down the temperature to 114° and set the timer for 6 to 8 or even 10 to 12 hours, depending on how crispy and crunchy you would like it to be.

Enjoy this with your lunch or as a snack. Stored it in an airtight glass jar, it will last from a few weeks up to a month or longer, depending on how long you dehydrate the food.

As with all of these recipes, after making it once, you may want to adjust it to your liking by adding a dash of coconut nectar, less orange rind or less juice, etc. Play with it, have fun, be creative!

"Clam" Chowder

This looks and tastes so much like clam chowder that it will RAWmaze you! Creamy comfort food at its best.

THEME: AMERICAN | SERVINGS: 2

INGREDIENTS

1 1/2 Cup Organic Cauliflower tops

4 Organic Brazil Nuts

1/2 Organic Lemon, juiced

1 Teaspoon Ginger, grated or chopped

4 Tablespoons Miso Master Organic Chickpea

1/4 Cup Olive Oil

3 Cups Water

Basil and Rosemary to taste, finely chopped

1 Teaspoon Maine Coast Sea Vegetables Company's Kelp Granules with Cayenne Pepper

Few Kalamata olives, sliced into small wheels then sliced in half

Few small Organic Pineapple chunks

Sea Salt to taste

DIRECTIONS:

Place all ingredients in the blender except for the olives and pineapple, and blend until smooth. Garnish with the sliced olives and pineapple and serve.

Cream of Broccoli Soup

I love soups, especially on chilly days. These soups can be warmed up to about 114 degrees and still be raw, living soups! There is a nutrient in broccoli that helps to burn stomach and belly fat, as well as helping your body deal with air pollution, so eating more broccoli is always a good, healthy idea! This recipe makes it easy and delicious.

THEME: AMERICAN | SERVINGS: 2-3

INGREDIENTS

3 to 4 small heads Organic Broccoli

1/4 Cup Olive Oil

2 to 3 Tablespoons Miso Master Organic Chickpea Miso

Sea Salt to taste

4 Cups water

1/4 Cup Raw Organic Brazil, Pine or Macadamia Nuts

1 Organic Avocado (optional)

DIRECTIONS:

Blend all ingredients to desired consistency. If you use the avocado for a creamier soup, you can eliminate the nuts. Drizzle a little olive oil and pomegranate seeds for garnish (see photos), and serve! I've found a new bowl made of fallen leaves, the most eco-green possible. Being a Eco Chef also means reusing and recycling, so I also use the avocado shell as a serving bowl, a playful way to present the broccoli soup.

Carrot Ginger Soup

I like the color and spice of this soup. It is great on cold or chilly days to warm up your spirit. Blended foods are healthy because they allow your digestive system to rest and makes nutrient absorption complete.

THEME: AMERICAN
SERVINGS: 2-3

INGREDIENTS

2 Large Grated Organic Carrots

1 Tablespoon Ginger, grated or chopped

3 Tablespoons Miso Master Organic Chickpea Miso

1/4 Cup Olive Oil

3 Cups Water

Rosemary to taste, finely chopped

Red Hot Chili Peppers (optional) for extra spice!

Sea Salt to taste

DIRECTIONS:

Pour the water in the blender first, then add the rest of the ingredients and blend until smooth, or the desired consistency then serve in bowls or cups. In the photograph I used a special "spiralizer" machine to grate the carrots into the "ribbons" and I chopped some organic green onions as a fun garnish!

I had a special Raw Living Food dinner in Hollywood with one of my favorite bands in the world, the Red Hot Chili Peppers. (Anthony and Flea, you rock!)

Creamy Tomato Soup

This is one of the most creamy and rejuvenating soups on the planet. All of these soups are very easy and take only a few minutes to prepare. I find that adding sunflower sprouts on top of any soup gives a sense of "noodle," tastes great, and is a great complimentary garnish. You can also add chopped baby spinach, slices of avocado or red bell peppers for garnish. This velvety tomato soup is very popular.

THEME: AMERICAN
SERVINGS: 2

INGREDIENTS

4 Roma or 2 regular Tomatoes

4 to 5 Pieces Sundried Tomatoes, soaked for 20 minutes in water

3 Tablespoons Miso Master Organic Chickpea Miso

1/3 Cup Olive Oil

3 Cups Water

Basil and Rosemary to taste, finely chopped

Maine Coast Sea Vegetables Company's Kelp Granules with Cayenne Pepper (optional)

Sea Salt to taste

DIRECTIONS:

Blend all the ingredients until smooth.

Serve with extra dulse granules and cayenne, olive oil and your choice of garnishes. We use and recommend Main Coast Sea Vegetables Company's Kelp Granules with Cayenne Pepper often, because kelp has a good amount of minerals we normally don't get unless we eat seaweed. Cayenne pepper helps to increase digestion and circulation, and both add flavor and depth to our foods as well.

Honeydew & Cucumber Soup

This is a sweet dessert soup that is best chilled or used to keep you cool. The combination of honeydew and cucumber is super refreshing and delightful!

THEME: AMERICAN | SERVINGS: 2–3

INGREDIENTS

1 Organic Honeydew Melon

1 Organic Cucumber

3 Cups Pure Water

Few teaspoons of Coconut Nectar

Organic Mint Garnish

DIRECTIONS:

Pour the water into the blender first, then add the melon and cucumber. Blend until smooth or desired consistency, then pour into serving bowls and enjoy!

Coconut nectar is optional.

Garnish with sliced cucumber and mint or dill (see photo).

SOUPS

RAW STAR RECIPES

Japanese Ramen Noodles

I hope you enjoy this new creation! I use an innovative kombucha technique that gives the raw noodles an amazing "cooked" taste and adds beneficial enzymes and probiotics for your good health!

THEME: JAPANESE | SERVINGS: 2–3

INGREDIENTS

1 Organic Butternut Squash (Substitute Yams if Squash is not available)

1 Young Coconut

1 Organic Persimmon (Substitute Mango or Papaya)

1 Organic Radish

1 Bottle of Organic Kombucha

Organic Fresh Basil and Chives for garnish

Organic Red Spicy Peppers and Seaweed for garnish (optional)

DIRECTIONS:

Use my signature series RAW STAR ceramic peeler to first peel the butternut squash, then make thin slices of the squash. Place slices on a wooden or bamboo cutting board. (Never use plastic cutting boards, the plastic gets into your food.) To make the very fine and thin "rawmen noodles", I suggest using my 8" Ceramic Knife for precision cuts, or a spiralizer. Slice the shaved slices into the finest "noodles" you can.

Pour a bottle of kombucha into a serving bowl and add your sliced noodles. Allow them to marinate as long as possible; it is best if you can cover and allow to soak in the fridge overnight. The next day it will have a "cooked" consistency!

When the noodles are ready, open a young coconut and carve out the "meat" into a boiled egg shape (see Bacon & Eggs). Do the same with the persimmon for the "yolk," top with garnish and serve.

Pho

Using chickpea miso as the soup base and a variety of your favorite vegetables makes a Vegan Raw Organic Pho come to life! You can also use kelp noodles for fun, but just the veggies and hot peppers work well in this traditional favorite.

THEME: VIETNAMESE | SERVINGS: 2–3

INGREDIENTS

1 Organic Purple Cabbage

1 Organic White Cabbage

1 Organic Napa Cabbage

1/2 Organic Daikon

1 Organic Carrot

1 Cup Organic Mung Bean Sprouts

Grated Organic Ginger (optional)

1 Organic Lime, juiced

3 to 4 Tablespoons Miso Master Organic Chickpea Miso

Organic Olive Oil to taste (optional)

DIRECTIONS:

This tastes best when warm; you can heat some water to 114° or serve at room temperature.

Add the hot water to a serving bowl and mix with a few tablespoons of chickpea miso to desired flavor.

Slice the 3 cabbages into very fine, thin "noodles," using a ceramic knife to keep it from wilting and keep it fresher longer.

Daikon is usually large, so you will need 1/2 or less. To make daikon noodles, use a spiralizer or any sort of vegetable "noodle" maker on "angel hair" setting, or you can hand-cut your own noodle shapes. (see photo) Daikon noodles resemble rice noodles. Add these to your miso soup bowl.

Use the RAW STAR Ceramic Peeler to "shave" or "peel" the carrots into thin noodle shapes, and add to the bowl. Add the sprouts, grated ginger, squeeze some lime and serve!

Note: A hand machine works best in this situation, making perfectly shaped noodles quickly and easily. I use a Japanese one from Sur La Table that makes the best noodle shapes. Sur La Table also has a online store.

Spicy Avocado Soup

This soup is smooth, nice and spicy. It can be used as a salad dressing as well, by adding a little more olive oil and a few teaspoons of coconut nectar to taste.

THEME: AMERICAN
SERVINGS: 2-3

INGREDIENTS

2 Organic Avocados

4 Tablespoons Miso Master Organic Chickpea Miso

1/4 Cup Olive Oil

3 Cups Water

1 Lime, juiced

Basil, Cilantro and Rosemary to taste, finely chopped

1/2 Hot Chili Pepper

Sea Salt to taste

DIRECTIONS:

Place all the ingredients in the blender and blend until smooth. This soup has such a great creamy, spicy flavor, perfect for winter or chilly days. For extra color and flavor you can add grated carrots or pieces of purple cabbage before blending.

Variation: To make a spicy Broccoli Soup, add a few broccoli tops before blending.

Thai Coconut Soup

I love Thai Cuisine for its spicy, colorful, exotic flavors. Thai cuisine is gaining popularity around the world for its spicy, vibrant tastes. I've been getting a lot of requests for this specially guarded secret recipe, so here it is!

THEME: THAI
SERVINGS: 2-3,

INGREDIENTS

1 Fresh Young Coconut, both the water and carefully scraped coconut flesh

Organic Carrots, grated

Zucchini

Small pieces of purple cabbage

1 Organic Lime, juiced

1 Teaspoon Ginger, grated or chopped

3 to 4 Tablespoons Miso Master Organic Chickpea Miso

1/4 Cup Organic Olive Oil

3 Cups Water

Organic Basil, Cilantro and Rosemary to taste, finely chopped

Sea Salt to taste

1/2 Hot Chili Pepper for extra spicy flavor (optional)

Small Organic Pineapple chunks

DIRECTIONS:

Pour the water into the blender first, then the coconut meat and coconut water, olive oil, lime juice and miso. Sprinkle sea salt to taste, then blend until very smooth.

Pour into serving serving bowls and add the rest of the chopped ingredients and garnishes

SOUPS

Waldorf Salad with "Mayo" Dressing

I was at a party where people wanted to make a Raw Organic Waldorf Salad, so we came up with a really quick "mayo" dressing and the salad turned out to be amazing! I added some raw touches to the classic famous Waldorf Salad recipe, enjoy!

THEME: AMERICAN | SERVINGS: 3–4

INGREDIENTS

2 to 3 Diced Organic Green Apples with skin

1 Tablespoon Organic Lemon Juice

2/3 Cup Organic Raisins (Franny's are the best!)

2/3 Cup Organic Celery, chopped

2/3 Cup Raw Organic Walnuts

1/3 Cup Sundried Organic Cranberries

RAW "MAYONNAISE":

1/3 Cup Organic Olive Oil

1/3 Cup Water

2/3 Cup Raw Organic Pine Nuts

Few Raw Organic Macadamia or Brazil Nuts (optional)

A little Organic Coconut Oil (optional)

3 Teaspoons Coconut Nectar

DIRECTIONS:

Chop and mix all the salad ingredients, place in a bowl, and sprinkle with sundried cranberries if you can get them.

Blend all "mayonnaise" ingredients until smooth. Pour on top of the ingredients, mix well, serve and enjoy. Simply delicious!

Please make sure you refrigerate leftover dressings. Some pressure or fermentation may occur in the dressing if you allow it to sit at room temperature, so be sure to release any built-up pressure and to refrigerate leftovers promptly.

SALAD

Red Lava Dressing

A nice red lava-like spread and dressing. Hawaii is the inspiration for this recipe, with its live lava flows that are constantly creating new parts of the Island. Something about the bright red color of lava and red bell peppers is very attractive and magical.

THEME: HAWAIIAN | SERVINGS: 2

INGREDIENTS

1 Organic Red Bell Pepper

1 Cup Soaked Raw Organic Almonds, Pine or Brazil Nuts

1 Tablespoon Miso Master Organic Chickpea Miso

1/4 Cup Organic Lemon Juice

Organic Basil or Rosemary or your favorite fresh herb, chopped

1 Tablespoon Coconut Nectar

Sea Salt to taste

DIRECTIONS:

I love the red lava-like color of this recipe! Soak your nuts of choice overnight, for easy preparation.

Seed the red bell pepper and blend it with the rest of the ingredients until super smooth. It will thicken after blending.

You can use Red Lava Dressing as a spread in lettuce wraps or on tacos, enchiladas, tostadas, etc.

To make a salad dressing, add 1/2 cup of water, 2 tablespoons of miso and 1/2 cup of olive oil. You can also add some Hawaiian pineapple chunks before blending, for a real luau flavor.

Please make sure you refrigerate leftover dressings. Some pressure or fermentation may occur in the dressing if you allow it to sit at room temperature, so be sure to release any built-up pressure and to refrigerate leftovers promptly.

Orange Delight Dressing

This dressing is light, simple, summery and refreshing with only three ingredients. Pour over your favorite light salad or dress up some sprouts for a snack.

THEME: AMERICAN
SERVINGS: 2–3

INGREDIENTS

2 Oranges, juiced

1 Cup Organic Olive Oil

1 Tablespoon Miso Master Organic Chickpea Miso (optional)

DIRECTIONS:

Mix the ingredients in a bowl or blender and serve over salad or veggies.

Variations: Blend dressing with 1/3 cup soaked sunflower seeds, pine nuts or soaked almonds for a creamy dressing or dip.

Please make sure you refrigerate leftover dressings. Some pressure or fermentation may occur in the dressing if you allow it to sit at room temperature, so be sure to release any built-up pressure and to refrigerate leftovers promptly.

Island Mango Dressing

Hawaii has a very special place in my heart because of all the fantastic adventures and friends I have there. You can find mangoes growing on public streets and people will give them away for free in boxes. There is an Aloha community spirit that I truly love about Hawaii, literally a "Fantasy Island" in many ways. Now we can share in the fantasy and transport ourselves to a tropical paradise with this dressing!

THEME: HAWAIIAN
SERVINGS: 2–3

INGREDIENTS

1 Ripe Organic Mango

1 Tablespoon Organic Ginger, finely chopped

1/4 Cup Water

1/3 Cup Organic Olive Oil to taste

1 Tablespoon Miso Master Organic Chickpea Miso

1 Tablespoon Coconut Nectar

DIRECTIONS:

Pour the water in blender first, then add the rest of the ingredients and blend until smooth. You may substitute fresh apple juice for the water. Nice, sweet, Island Mango Dressing to remind you of PA~RAW~DISE!

Organic food is such a blessing; if you enjoy it in the right ways, more miracles will manifest on many levels. I have seen this happen for many people and in my own life.

Tropical foods and recipes can instantly take you to a Island realm that is dreamy and delightful! With this dressing, Hawaii and PA~RAW~DISE does not seem so far away.

Sweet Mustard Dressing

Everyone loves the sweet-and-sour taste of sweet mustard dressings. This one is low in the glycemic index, with less sugar and the ultimate in health. Tangy and tasty! People actually e-mail to thank me or to tell me how popular this is at parties, which makes me very happy!

THEME: AMERICAN | SERVINGS: 2–3

INGREDIENTS

1/2 Cup Organic Olive Oil

1/4 Cup Water

1 Teaspoon dry Mustard or Horseradish

Few pieces Purple Cabbage (optional)

1 Tablespoon Miso Master Organic Chickpea Miso

3 Coconut Nectar

5 Soaked Raw Organic Almonds or 1/4 Cup Pine Nuts

1/4 Cup Bragg's Raw Organic Apple Cider Vinegar

Sea Salt to taste

DIRECTIONS:

Put all the ingredients in the blender and blend until smooth. The dressing has a nice sweet-and-sour taste that goes well over a cucumber or green papaya salad.

Please make sure you refrigerate leftover dressings. Some pressure or fermentation may occur in the dressing if you allow it to sit at room temperature, so be sure to release any built-up pressure and to refrigerate leftovers promptly.

Ranch Dressing

Just think, a Raw Organic Vegan Ranch Dressing that is super-creamy and decadent-tasting, the smoothest ranch dressing ever! No preservatives, dairy free, no MSG, no chemicals, all organic, fresh, healthy, you deserve the best!

THEME: AMERICAN | SERVINGS: 2

INGREDIENTS

1 Cup Water

1 Cup Raw Organic Almonds (soaked overnight in clean water, in a covered bowl)

Coconut Nectar

2 Tablespoons Lemon juice

2 to 3 Tablespoons Organic Olive Oil

Sea Salt to taste

Organic Rosemary and Basil, finely chopped

Organic Carrots, grated

Red & Yellow Bell Peppers, chopped small

Cucumbers

Purple Cabbage pieces

DIRECTIONS:

Blend the almonds and water in the until very smooth. Place in a bowl and mix in the rest of the chopped ingredients, seasonings and lemon juice. Serve or store unused portions in the refrigerator, not at room temperature. This dressing is so creamy on salads and sprout salads, a personal favorite.

Raw Organic Ketchup

Ketchup is a world classic favorite. Now you can make your own fresh Raw Organic version at home in just minutes! Nothing is better than a homemade version that is quick, simple and delightful. Goes perfectly with the Onion Rings, "Sunburger" and other recipes in this book.

THEME: AMERICAN | SERVINGS: 2–3

INGREDIENTS

2 Organic Tomatoes, chopped

1/4 Cup Raw Organic Bragg's Apple Cider Vinegar

1/4 Cup Organic Sundried Tomatoes, soaked

Dash of Coconut Nectar

Sea Salt to taste

DIRECTIONS:

Blend all of the ingredients and pour into a serving bowl or container.

Coconut Vanilla Fruit Pie with Chocolate Crust

This super-creamy Coconut Pie reminds me of the sun and fresh ocean breezes of the islands. Its refreshingly smoothness will transport you to a Island Paradise. The chocolate crust perfectly compliments the decadent creaminess of the coconut and fruit filling.

THEME: AMERICAN | SERVINGS: 2–3

INGREDIENTS

CRUST:

1 Cup Raw Organic Sunflower Seeds

4 to 5 teaspoons Coconut Nectar

1/2 Cup Carob Powder

Dash of Organic Cinnamon(optional)

FILLING:

1/2 Vanilla Bean, cut and scraped, using only the insides (discard the skin)

1/2 Cup Coconut Oil

1/2 Cup Pine Nuts

Dash of Vanilla Extract

1/4 Golden Organic Flax Seeds, ground (natural thickener, optional)

1/4 Cup Water

1 to 2 teaspoons Coconut Nectar

FRUIT:

Organic Peaches, Kiwi, Strawberry, Raspberry, Blueberry, or your favorite fruit.

DIRECTIONS:

Blend the sunflower seeds to sand consistency and put in a large bowl. Mix in the rest of the crust ingredients until well coated, then shape into your favorite cake or pie mold.

Blend all filling ingredient, water first, until really smooth. Pour into crust. Put in the fridge or freezer until firm.

Add sliced and chopped fruit artistically to the top, and serve!

Note: You can serve it right away but it will be very soft. Chilling allows it to become firm. You can add ground flax seeds to give the coconut filling more body.

Raspberry Chocolate Cinnamon Crumb Cake

This is a very fancy and gourmet-looking and -tasting dessert. It gives the impression that you spent hours in the kitchen, but should only take you 5 to 10 minutes to make before and is ready to serve, eat and enjoy! t So simple, a child can make it. To think that totally decadent new dessert recipes are actually good for you and for the planet, it is all possible with Eco Chef Bryan Au's recipes!

THEME: AMERICAN | SERVINGS: 2–3

INGREDIENTS

1 Organic Banana

1 Cup Raw Organic Golden Flax Seeds, grounded (or Flax USA pre-ground)

2 to 3 Teaspoons Coconut Nectar

4 to 6 Tablespoons Raw Organic Carob Powder, adjust to taste

Organic Orange Zest for garnish

5 Organic Raspberries

Few dashes of Organic Cinnamon to taste

"CHOCOLATE" FROSTING:

3 Tablespoons Carob Powder

1 to 2 Tablespoons Coconut Nectar

DIRECTIONS:

Peel the banana, place in a large mixing bowl, and use a fork to mash it by hand. Add the flax seed and the carob powders then pour in coconut nectar, mixing until well blended. Adjust the amount of carob powder to taste. Add more ground flax for a firm cake, and less for a moist cake.

Grease a small round pastry cylinder with coconut oil. Press the dough into 1/2 of the cylinder, add 4 raspberries, then put more dough on top, setting aside a bit of dough to make cinnamon crumbs.

Carefully press on the dough and lift the cylinder so that the cake is sitting in one piece on the plate. This may take some practice!

Make the frosting by hand-mixing carob powder in a bowl with coconut nectar, and drizzle over the cake, top and sides.

Put the reserved dough in a mixing bowl, add cinnamon and hand mix well. With your fingers, make little crumb-sized balls and add these to the top of the cake. Zest some orange for the top of the cake and garnish with mint (see photo).

Watch your guests' delight at this beautiful presentation and its extravagantly rich taste!

This recipe makes one medium chocolate cake or 2 small chocolate cakes, depending on your size of pastry cylinder.

Equipment Note: You can purchase the pastry cylinder at any chef or restaurant supply store. I like to shop at Sur La Table, as they have everything at great prices and a online store as well.

Triple Layer Chocolate Cake

This one is for all of you chocolate lovers out there! What else is dessert for? Chocolate, of course! We use Raw Organic Carob Powder in this healthy, decadent recipe for your enjoyment and health. It looks and tastes just like chocolate, but with super all-natural health benefits.

THEME: AMERICAN | SERVINGS: 2–3

INGREDIENTS

1 Fresh Young Coconut, meat carefully scraped out

1 Tablespoon Organic Virgin Coconut Oil

4 Tablespoons Coconut Nectar

1/4 Cup Water

1/2 Cup Raw Organic Pine Nuts

2-3 Tablespoons Coconut Nectar

Soaked Almond Pulp from Almond Milk Recipe mixed with 1/4 Cup of either Coconut Nectar, blended Raisin water or Date water.

Raw Organic Carob Powder to taste

Organic Cinnamon to taste

Variation: Substitute Pine Nuts for Almond Pulp, hand-mixing 1/2 Cup Raw Organic Golden Flax Seeds, ground, 1 Banana, mashed, and 1/4 Cup Coconut Nectar

DIRECTIONS:

This will be the quickest triple layer chocolate cake you will ever make, and the most decadent and scrumptious cake too, most of it will be living and will connect you with true health and beauty. (You save so much time by not baking it!)

Mix carob powder with almond pulp to the desired level of chocolateness, then add some of the coconut nectar. Press with a spoon into several round glass serving containers.

Blend water, pine nuts and coconut nectar, then add carob powder to taste, about 2 to 3 tablespoons is the suggested amount. Pour over the almond pulp to form the 2nd layer.

Blend water, coconut meat, coconut oil, coconut nectar (or homemade sweetener of raisins or pitted dates blended with water); add carob powder and blend until smooth. Pour to form the 3rd layer. Sprinkle with a little cinnamon.

You can either serve it now or allow it to chill in the fridge until firm before serving.

For a fancy gourmet presentation, make round cookie-cutter shapes of paper and tape. (Gourmet chefs use a clear biodegradable corn plastic, taping it to make a tubular shape.) Place in the middle of a plate and fill with the 3 different layers. Allow to chill and firm in the fridge, then cut the tape or carefully remove the paper or biodegradable corn plastic, and serve.

Variations: Use your imagination and creativity!

Create different layers and flavor combinations, such as a carob almond layer topped with a mango cheesecake layer, or try the strawberry cream pie mixture as a layer.

Add blackberries, raspberries or strawberries between the layers to make a black forest type of dessert cake.

5 Minute Chocolate Cake

Flourless and dairy-free Chocolate Cakes are quite fashionable and trendy. Here is a Raw Organic version that is so fresh and delicious, you will love it! Chocolate lovers will really enjoy this surprising new Eco Chef recipe. A real and healthy treat that is quick and easy.

THEME: AMERICAN | SERVINGS: 5–6

INGREDIENTS

2 Organic Bananas

1 Cup Raw Organic Golden Flax Seeds, grounded (or Flax USA pre-ground)

2 to 3 Teaspoons Coconut Nectar

4 to 6 Tablespoons Raw Organic Carob Powder, adjusting to taste

2-3 Tablespoons Coconut Nectar

"CHOCOLATE" FROSTING:

4 Tablespoons Carob Powder

3 Tablespoons Coconut Nectar

GARNISH:

Strawberries or other favorite Berries or Fruit, Chopped Raw Organic Almonds, Brazil Nuts Organic Cinnamon (optional)

DIRECTIONS:

Peel the bananas and place in a large mixing bowl, mashing by hand with a fork. Add flax seed and carob powders. Pour in coconut nectar and hand mix with a fork until well blended. Adjust the amount of carob powder to taste; add more ground flax for a firm cake and less for a moist cake.

Grease a medium cake pan or 2 small cake pans with coconut oil. Press the dough into the cake, then flip onto a serving plate.

In a medium bowl, hand mix coconut nectar with carob powder until it is well mixed and acts like a sauce or frosting, then drizzle or cover the top of the chocolate cake.

Garnish with fresh organic strawberries, berries, your favorite fruit or chopped nuts. Sprinkle with cinnamon and enjoy!

Candied Apples

People ask me for fun holiday Raw Organic recipes all the time and I always come up with something, because I am here to make people happy and healthy! This is a super-fun recipe that kids and adults both love...and it only takes about 2 minutes for each Candied Apple!

THEME: AMERICAN | SERVINGS: 3–4

INGREDIENTS

3 to 4 Organic Gala Apples

Raw Organic Walnuts, Almonds, Pecans

7 Tablespoons Coconut Nectar

1 Cup Raw Organic Carob Powder

2-3 Tablespoons Coconut nectar

Drink Mixing Sticks or Chopsticks for the Apple

DIRECTIONS:

I find Gala to work best but use your favorite type of apple. Wash and dry the apples. Push a mixing stick or chopstick into the top of the apple for a handle.

In a large mixing bowl, combine carob powder with the coconut nectar, mixing by hand with a fork until you get the desired consistency; less coconut nectar for a thicker "Chocolate Sauce" and more for a softer, liquid sauce.

Use a spoon to coat the apples, then chop the nuts, sprinkle around the sauce and serve.

Kids and adults love this fun and easy recipe, so delicious while remaining low in sugar.

Enjoy the holidays and share the gifts of love, laughter and health with your friends, family and the world!

Strawberry Cream Pie

Strawberry is one of my favorite fruits! This recipe is sure to delight strawberry fans with its naturally sweet and organic bliss. I found the giant organic strawberries used in my recipes and photos at www.Calgiant.com.

THEME: AMERICAN | SERVINGS: 2–3

INGREDIENTS

2 Cups Organic Strawberries
(CalGiant.com)

1 1/2 Cups Raw Organic Brazil Nuts
or Raw Organic Almonds, soaked
or Sunflower Seeds or Pine Nuts,
soaked

1/4 Cup Coconut Nectar
or 2-3 Tablespoons Really Raw
Coconut nectar

1/4 Cup Water

1/4 Cup Goji Berries, soaked
(optional)

PIE CRUST:

1 to 2 cups Pistachio
or Sunflower Seeds
or Almonds, ground to powder

1/4 Coconut Nectar
or 2-3 Tablespoons Really Raw
Coconut nectar

DIRECTIONS:

This recipe can be made in several quick, easy ways:

- You can use the nuts to make a really decadent creamy strawberry cream pie, or if you don't have much time, just mash several bananas with the strawberries and coconut nectar for a quick dessert.

- Almond pulp and coconut nectar gives a more traditional-looking crust.

- Ground flax seeds with mashed banana makes a crust alternative.

- For dramatic gourmet creation, I recommend using pistachio nuts blended with coconut meat (optional) and coconut nectar for the crust. (You may also use a food processor.) Coconut meat will hold the crust together while making it creamier.

Mix ground pistachio or almond pulp by hand with coconut nectar (or homemade sweetener: raisins or dates blended with water) for the crust. Cover the bottom of a round glass pan with the mixture and press it down to make a crust.

Blend water, strawberries, your choice of nuts, and coconut nectar until smooth. Pour the Strawberry Cream over the crust and serve right away, or let chill for 1 hour in the refrigerator.

To make this strawberry cream pie an even more amazing superfood, add soaked goji berries just before blending the strawberry mixture. Use a few soaked goji berries as a garnish, along with sliced strawberries.

To make the strawberry cream thicker, add a few more nuts at a time while blending. I love how the bright green color of the pistachios contrasts with the pink color of the strawberries. This is a gourmet super dessert!

RAW STAR RECIPES

Crepes

A raw organic crepe? Is it possible? Yes, it is!

THEME: AMERICAN | SERVINGS: 2–3

INGREDIENTS

1 Cup Raw Organic Golden Flax Seeds (or Flax USA, preground)

5 Tablespoons Organic Coconut Oil in liquid form

6 Tablespoons Water

Coconut Nectar to taste

DIRECTIONS:

Grind the flax seeds to a fine powerder in the blender, or use pre-ground. Pour flax meal into a bowl, mix with the coconut oil and water by hand, using a fork, then use a spoon to press the mixture down to mix well. Make a medium-sized ball with your hands, press it onto plate with your hands, then use ,a spoon to form a very thin, round layer. Fill one side of the crepe with your favorite fruit, any of the dessert creams or fillings, then carefully roll the crepe.

You can use the carob "Chocolate Sauce," the second layer in the Triple Layer Chocolate Cake, more of your choice of dessert creams/fillings or just coconut nectar on top to make it sweet and complete! If you put guacamole or the nacho pine nut cheese sauce inside you will have a Raw Enchilada.

Goji Berry Macaroons

As I was creating all new Raw Organic Cuisine and dessert recipes, one of my yoga friends asked if I happened to have a macaroon cookie recipe, since it was her favorite. I didn't, but was able to invent one on the spot just for her and want to share it with you!

THEME: AMERICAN | SERVINGS: 3–4

INGREDIENTS

2 Fresh Young Coconuts

1/4 Cup Raw Organic Buckwheat Groats, soaked & blended (optional)

Almond Pulp (from Almond Milk Recipe) mixed with 1/4 Cup Coconut Nectar

4 Tablespoons Organic Virgin Coconut Oil

1/4 Cup Water

1/4 Cup Coconut Nectar

Few Soaked Goji Berries

Few Tablespoons Raw Organic Golden Flax Seeds, finely ground

DIRECTIONS:

These macaroons have so much flavor and energy that you will want to make a bunch. This recipe makes about 10 macaroons. You can make these with goji berries in the mix or just on top as a garnish.

Place all ingredients into a blender with the water first, coconut flesh next with some coconut water, almond pulp, coconut oil, then coconut nectar and soaked goji berries (optional). Blend to a semi-chunky consistency. When the coconut flesh is pretty fine and semi-smooth in texture, you know you are done blending.

Using your hands, make macaroon-sized balls and coat with extra almond pulp to make it drier and firmer. You can also use ground flax seeds or blended buckwheat (optional). Slightly flatten the macaroon balls with your hands or spoon, add one soaked goji berry on top for garnish, and enjoy!

These will be moist, which adds water to your body. Remember, the more water you add to your body, the more hydrated you become, which will naturally make you feel great.

If you can also be more "fluid" in your movements, you can improve your well being too. This is why I suggest practicing yoga. If you do yoga and eat Raw Organic Cuisine, you will find that you will turn into a superhero, and feel super good about it!

In the photo I used a zester to carefully zest and scrape some extra fresh coconut to add to the top of the cookies.

Blueberry Mousse Pie with Oatmeal Graham Crust

If you love blueberries as much as I do, you will truly enjoy this new, simple, creamy Raw dessert! It is so easy to make and a delicious crowd-pleasing recipe.

THEME: AMERICAN | SERVINGS: 2–3

INGREDIENTS

2 Organic Bananas

2 Cups Fresh Organic Blueberries

1/2 Cup Raisins

1/4 Cup Water

1 to 2 Cups Raw Organic Oats

1 1/4 Cup Raw Organic Golden Flax Seeds, ground (or FlaxUSA, preground)

Few dashes of Organic Cinnamon to taste

DIRECTIONS:

Blend the water and raisins to make a sweetener sauce; pour into a large mixing bowl, add the oats and hand mix until well coated. Add more oats to achieve a drier pie crust consistency, and mix in the ground flax seeds, which help keep the crust together. Sprinkle cinnamon to taste and press into a pie pan.

Blend the bananas, 3/4 of the blueberries, raisins and water until very smooth, then pour into pie crust. Add the rest of blueberries on top, chill in refrigerator for 10 to 15 minutes to firm, then serve. You can add more ground flax seeds to the filling when blending for a firmer set. Variation: add carob powder to crust to make it a chocolate crust.

I encourage you to play with this recipe (and any recipe!) and adjust it to your liking. Make a quick blueberry pie or small blueberry fruit tarts. Add more or less water, or more or less raisins in the crust. Try more blueberries, or less. Organic oats can be eaten raw, and are a trendy and healthy addition to cookies, pie crusts and desserts.

This cookbook is one of the ways that I contribute more health and harmony to the world in the most loving, caring, healing, joyful and fun ways possible. I love to help people in fun and wonderful ways. You can always ask me any questions by e-mailing me directly; I will answer your questions!

Pecan Pie

This is similar to the Blueberry Mousse Recipe, using pitted dates and banana for the filling. It looks and tastes just like a baked pecan pie but only takes a few minutes and is very delicious. A real festive treat!

THEME: AMERICAN | SERVINGS: 2–3

INGREDIENTS

1 Cup Raw Organic Pecans

2 Organic Bananas

1 Cup Organic Pitted Dates

1/2 Cup Raisins

1/4 Cup Water

1 to 2 Cups Raw Organic Oats

1 1/4 Cup Raw Organic Golden Flax Seeds, ground (or FlaxUSA preground)

Few dashes of Organic Cinnamon to taste

DIRECTIONS:

Blend the water and raisins to make a sweetener sauce; pour into a large mixing bowl, add the oats and hand mix until well coated. Add more oats to achieve a drier pie crust consistency, and mix in the ground flax seeds, which help keep the crust together. Sprinkle cinnamon to taste and press into a pie pan.

Blend bananas with pitted dates and a dash of cinnamon until very smooth, then pour into pie crust. Add pecans on top, arranged beautifully; chill in refrigerator for 10 to 15 minutes to let firm, then serve.

Variations:

- Add more ground flax seeds to the filling when blending, if you want it more firm.
- Blend pecans to a powder and add to the crust or the filling for more of a pecan flavor.
- Add carob powder to crust to make it a chocolate crust.

Fruit Danish

This is one of my newly invented recipes. These "pastries" are colorful, fruity and easy to make. I love danishes and now there is a super-healthy Raw Organic Vegan version that takes just a few minutes to make and needs no baking, preserving all the nutrients, vitamins, minerals and benefits. Finally, real "fast food" that is healthy, fun and nutritious!

THEME: AMERICAN | SERVINGS: 2–3

INGREDIENTS

3/4 Cup Raw Organic Oats

4 Tablespoons Raw Organic Golden Flax Seeds, ground (or FlaxUsa, preground)

6 Tablespoons Water

Pinch of Sea Salt

4 Tablespoons Organic Coconut Oil

2 to 3 Tablespoons Coconut Nectar (or your own sweetener, made of water blended with either raisins or pitted dates)

FRUIT FILLING:

1 Organic Orange or Peach

3 or 4 Organic Raspberries

4 to 5 Raw Organic Almonds, sliced or slivered

DIRECTIONS:

Make sure the coconut oil is melted or in liquid form; you can put it in the sun to melt if it is hardened.

In a large bowl, hand mix all "pastry" ingredients well. Using your hands, shape into desired Danish shapes and put on serving plate. Get creative with different shapes as well! (see photo)

Cut and peel the orange, peach, or your favorite fruit into wedges and place atop the Danish.

In a medium mixing bowl, crush the raspberries with a fork to add to the top of the Danish and use a whole raspberry as garnish. Chop the almonds carefully into slivers or slices for the final garnish, and enjoy!

Donuts

This amazing new no-fry donut recipe does not have to be dehydrated and contains no nuts! Many Raw recipes use nuts; however, I have been asked for no-nut recipes so folks can stay slim, trim and keep heir fat intake down to a minimum. Here it is, in the form of a donut!

THEME: AMERICAN | SERVINGS: 3–4

INGREDIENTS

2 Large Bananas

1 1/2 Cup Golden Flax Seeds

Coconut Nectar

TOPPINGS

Coconut Oil

Coconut Nectar

Raw Organic Carob Powder

Organic Cinnamon

DIRECTIONS:

Peel bananas and mash them with a fork in a large mixing bowl. Blend flax seeds until they are a very fine powder, then pour this into the bananas and mix until evenly coated, adjusting the amount of flax seeds for the desired moistness and firmness of the donuts. (Remember that as flax seeds are absorbed into the bananas, they will firm up. Depending on the size of the bananas used, please adjust accordingly.)

When the mixture is well mixed and you are satisfied with the consistency, form balls, poke a hole in the middle, and flatten slightly with your hand to form donuts. Place on a plate.

Glazed Donut: Drizzle some coconut nectar (optional), lightly coat with coconut oil, then drizzle a little more coconut nectar (optional).

Chocolate Donut: Mix carob powder with coconut nectar to make "Chocolate Sauce." Add a little water to make it glossy and lighter, then drizzle or coat the donut. For a thicker chocolate sauce, do not use extra water.

Cinnamon Donut: Llightly drizzle with coconut nectar, sprinkle cinnamon on top and serve!

This is a totally new fun, fast and healthy "donut"!

Pancakes

In the Raw Organic Cuisine world there are few Raw breakfast items, so I invented the Raw Organic Pancake! This ORIGINAL RECIPE, which I invented in 2005, is often duplicated and copied. I have 2 versions of pancakes: this one does not require a dehydrator, so it is fast and easy and the pancakes won't be warm.

This is a fresh and delicious way to start your day with healthy flax seeds, which have many health benefits, along with fresh fruit. Raw Organic Cuisine is all about eating more fresh, organic fruits and vegetables in fun new ways. These pancakes are quite satisfying and filling; they can be a bit "heavy," so you will only want to eat one. You can make a thinner version and roll into fruit crepes!

THEME: AMERICAN | SERVINGS: 2–3

INGREDIENTS

1 Cup Raw Organic Golden Flax Seeds (or Flax USA pre-ground)

4 Tablespoons Organic Coconut Oil in liquid form

2 Tablespoons Water

Coconut Nectar to taste

DIRECTIONS:

Blend the flax seeds into a powder, pour into a bowl and mix with the coconut oil and water, using a fork. Make sure to press down and mix very well until all the flax is coated and the whole mixture is really together.

Split the mixture in half, form a ball with your hands and flatten on a plate; do the same with the other half. Drizzle the pancake with coconut nectar (you can also make your own sweetener by blending raisins or pitted dates with water). Top with fruit and serve.

New coconut nectar is very healthy, with no sugar, low glycemic index, neutral Ph and living enzymes. You will feel amazingly healthy after trying it just once.

Cupcakes

Cupcakes are very popular again. Now we have a all new Raw Organic Vegan version to enjoy! We use the "donut" dough recipe for the cupcakes, what could be easier or healthier? Flax is very healthy, especially when blended in a powder form, which makes it easily digestible with many great benefits.

THEME: AMERICAN | SERVINGS: 2–3

INGREDIENTS

2 Large Organic Bananas

1 1/2 Cup Organic Golden Flax Seeds (or Flax USA pre-ground)

3 to 4 Tablespoons Coconut Nectar

TOPPINGS

Coconut Nectar

Coconut Oil

Carob Powder

Pistachio Nuts, Goji Berries, or Fruit and Nuts of your choice

DIRECTIONS:

"Dough": Peel bananas and mash them with a fork in a large mixing bowl. Blend flax seeds until they are a very fine powder, then pour this into the bananas and mix until evenly coated, adjusting the amount of flax seeds for the desired moistness and firmness of the donuts. (Remember that as flax seeds are absorbed into the bananas, they will firm up. Depending on the size of the bananas used, please adjust accordingly.)

Put the "dough" into fancy gold or paper cupcake cups, then embellish with your favorite toppings, such as coconut nectar or Carob Coconut Nectar "Chocolate Sauce" from the Donut recipe. (optional-the dough is already sweet) Or simply add coconut oil for "frosting," add fruit and serve! (In hot areas the coconut oil may melt, so you may want to refrigerate the coconut oil first)

The "sprinkles" (see photo) are chopped pistachio nuts and goji berries.

Hot Pancakes

This is the hot version of my pancake recipe. These Raw Organic Pancakes are actually hot and fluffy right out of the dehydrator! Soaked almonds add more living nutrition and health to this recipe. Most of my recipes are not dehydrated, but in the Raw Organic Cuisine world we do enjoy some dehydrated recipes and foods for fun. The dehydrator warms food slowly at a low temperature; the food is still considered to be Raw as the living enzymes, nutrition and nutrients are retained, which is the point of this fun new cuisine and lifestyle.

THEME: AMERICAN | SERVINGS: 2–3

INGREDIENTS

3 Tablespoons Raw Organic Almonds, soaked for 1 day and rinsed with fresh water

3 Tablespoons Almond Milk

3 Tablespoons Almond Pulp (from Almond Milk recipe)

3 Tablespoons Raw Organic Golden Flax Seeds, ground (or FlaxUSA pre-ground)

3 Tablespoons Coconut Nectar

3 Tablespoons Water

Few Organic Blueberries, Raspberry and Bananas for garnish

ALMOND MILK:

2 Cups Water

1 Cup Raw Organic Almonds (Soaked or not soaked)

DIRECTIONS:

With clean, pure water in a dry, clean area, soak raw almonds for a day. (Do not refrigerate during soaking; because the low temperature will prevent the sprouting and activation process of the enzymes and nutrients that we are trying to achieve.)

Rinse the almonds in clean water and blend with water until smooth. Using a strainer or a cheesecloth, strain and drain the mixture into a large mixing bowl, so that you have almond milk and almond pulp.

In large bowl, add the 3 tablespoons of each ingredient and hand-mix very well. Pour or spoon the batter into round pancake shapes on to the Teflex sheets on the trays included in the Good4U Dehydrator. (Please look at the photos as a guide.) Turn the dehydrator to the highest temperature, then in the next ten minutes lower the temperature slowly to 114° for 8 to 10 hours on the timer.

After about 4 hours of dehydrating, flip the pancakes and remove the Teflex sheets so that both sides are evenly dehydrated. In another 4 to 6 hours the recipe will be done and ready to enjoy. When serving, garnish with organic blueberries, bananas, strawberries and your favorite fruit.

Dehydrating times vary according to where you live, weather, humidity and elevation, so please adjust times and check on the food, to your desired consistency and taste. In fact, please adjust *all* of my Eco Chef recipes to your liking and taste; some recipes will take a few tries to get them just the way you like it.

Note on Dehydrating: When using a dehydrator, we raise the temperature very high in the beginning in order to prevent any mold or fungus from growing on the food in the warm, moist environment, then we slowly lower it to 114° to keep the food raw and maintain the living beneficial enzymes, nutrients, vitamins and minerals intact.

The concern in dehydrating at low temperatures is that microscopic mold and fungus can grow in the food undetectably and if you eat it, it might increase the amount of mold, fungus or candida in your body. To prevent this, you simply turn up the temperature to the highest then in 10 minutes slowly lower it to 114° and everything is perfect! This method is recommended by Gabriel Cousens' research in optimal dehydrated foods; all dehydrated foods should be made with this important technique.

"Oatmeal or Cereal & Milk"

This is a favorite breakfast and snack. This recipe takes just 5 minutes to make and is creamy, delicious and very healthy. We use Almond Pulp and Almond Milk made for this recipe in many other recipes and desserts, so please save these. Another great way to start your day!

THEME: AMERICAN | SERVINGS: 2–3

INGREDIENTS

OATMEAL AND CEREAL:

2 Cups Organic Golden Flax Seeds
(or Flax USA pre-ground)

ALMOND MILK:

1 Cup Almonds, soaked

3 Cups Water

2 to 3 Tablespoons Coconut Nectar
(optional)

Cinnamon (optional)

DIRECTIONS:

Almond Milk: Pour the water first into the blender, then the soaked almonds with a bit of coconut nectar to sweeten and blend, until the almonds become small crumbs in size. Strain into a large bowl using cheesecloth to make almond milk; save the almond pulp to make RAW cookies, pie shells, desserts and more! Set aside the almond milk for use in smoothies, the Chocolate Shake Recipe and more.

Oatmeal and Cereal: Blend flax seeds to a fine powder, about 5 minutes. (It is a lot easier to use the FlaxUSA pre-ground.) Put the flax seed powder into a bowl, add the almond milk and stir slightly. This looks and tastes like cooked oatmeal or a breakfast cereal, but is totally vegan, Organic and RAW!

You can add your favorite fruit to your cereal: blueberries, strawberries, soaked goji berries or cinnamon. Yum!

Golden flax has an incredible energy with healing properties. Flaxseed oil, which is usually very expensive in the health food store, has amazing power. Now you can get all the benefits, as ground flax seeds are easier for the body to digest. Almond Milk has great enzymes and nutrition as well. This is a quick and easy Raw breakfast treat!

Raw Organic breakfast recipes that look and taste like the "cooked" version are rare, not easy to come by. Use leftover Almond Pulp to make the amazing desserts, cookies and pie shell crusts in other recipes and chapters.

The point of making our food RAW is for the all-natural vitamins, minerals, enzymes and benefits, intact for maximum health benefits and value. You will feel energized, and experience many benefits that will encourage you to go further with the Raw Organic Cuisine enjoyed by millions of people. Many people love Raw Organic food, snacks and desserts; they feel instantly healthier, happier and more alive, and are able to anti-age naturally.

RAW STAR RECIPES

RAWs'mores!

From a cooked inorganic dessert to a healthy, fun, raw organic dessert, RAWmazingly RAWlicious RAWsmores are a snack treat with great health benefits. Now "junk food" and "fast food" is actually good for you! The planet thanks you for trying my new recipes and techniques.

THEME: AMERICAN | SERVINGS: 3–4

INGREDIENTS

1 Organic Banana

1/2 Cup Raw Organic Golden Flax Seeds, ground (or FlaxUSA pre-ground)

2 to 3 Tablespoons Raw Organic Coconut Oil

2 Tablespoons Coconut Nectar

Organic Cinnamon to taste

3 to 4 Tablespoons Raw Organic Carob Powder

DIRECTIONS:

This recipe is so quick and easy to make, and really does taste like a S'more!

In a large mixing bowl combine ground flax seeds and cinnamon to taste with the crushed banana. Mix well with a fork, adding more ground flax if it is too wet, or perhaps less banana. Using your hands, form small squares and set aside on a plate.

In a medium mixing bowl, combine coconut nectar with carob powder to make a thick "chocolate sauce."

Using a spoon and your hands, make marshmallow-like shapes with the raw organic coconut oil and place it on one of the squares. Using a spoon, put some of the chocolate sauce on the coconut oil and some on the square, and assemble to form the RAWs'mores.

Put chopsticks through the RAWs'mores for a fun presentation, or just use your hands and eat it as is. This is a very fun and easy recipe to make and it tastes RAWmazing! Please use the photos as a guide.

Baklava

Baklava is my favorite so I had to create this all new Raw Organic version, which is extra refreshing and has a nice, light, sweet quality. It is so simple and easy too. This should only take 5 minutes to make. Enjoy!

THEME: MEDITERRANEAN | SERVINGS: 4–5

INGREDIENTS

1 Medium Organic Fuji Apple

1 Cup Raw Organic Sunflower Seeds
or Walnuts
or Pistachios

2 Tablespoons Coconut Nectar

DIRECTIONS:

Carefully slice the Fuji apple into 4 very thin slices. Stack the 4 layers on top of each other on a plate and carefully cut into a square shape with a knife.

Blend your choice of nuts until they are very small crumb sized. Baklavas have different nuts; sunflower seeds have the best price and taste for this recipe. You may soak the nuts overnight in water to activate their nutrients and enzymes, but I find that unsoaked ones make this more crunchy. Experiment!

Pour the nut meal into a bowl and mix with coconut nectar until well blended. Using your hands or a spoon, fill between each layer of apples with the coconut nectar-nut mixture and pat down with a spoon to compact before adding the next layer on top. Fill all the layers, drizzle with more coconut nectar on top, and enjoy!

People are amazed that this looks and tastes like the baked Baklava version, but fresher and lighter. I have been told that it is the best dessert ever! Sometimes the most simple recipes truly are the best.

Chocolate Truffles & Bon Bons

RAW Organic Chocolates are a new popular trend. These are so good, and actually healthy for you in moderation. We use carob powder because it is inexpensive and easy, tastes like chocolate and is a little healthier too. Now you can make your own chocolates at home, just the way you like them. Some people have even turned this into a business!

THEME: AMERICAN | SERVINGS: 3–4

INGREDIENTS

3 to 4 Tablespoons Organic Cacao Butter (Order cacao butter online or from your local health food store or Whole Foods Market)

3 Tablespoons Raw Organic Carob Powder
or Cacao Nibs, blended to powder

1 to 2 Tablespoons Coconut Nectar

2 to 3 Tablespoons Organic Coconut Oil

DIRECTIONS:

The first step is to grate or grind the cacao butter then melt it, either by using the sun or on the stove, using very little flame. It melts very quickly; be careful to heat just to the melting point and stop. You want it to be in a liquid state.

The same goes for the coconut oil. Use the coconut oil if you want your chocolates to be more of a "milk chocolate" flavor; without coconut oil, it is a more of a "dark chocolate."

Add all ingredients to a blender and blend until very smooth. Pour into favorite chocolate molds, top as you wish, and refrigerate or put in freezer until just hardened.

Variations and suggestions:

- Cover pitted cherries, goji berries, nuts or strawberries to make bon bons.

- If you don't want to use cacao butter you can still make the recipe. Cacao butter keeps the chocolate stable at room temperature. Without it, melting can occur.

- Get creative and experiment with different measurements of the recipe, create some amazing chocolate truffles and bon bons with different fillings, fruits, get creative!

- Another simple recipe and technique is to melt coconut oil into liquid form and blend until smooth with carob powder and a sweetener such as coconut nectar, or raisins or pitted dates blended with water. Pour into molds and put into the freezer until it just reaches hardened consistency.

Mint Chocolate Mousse

Everyone loves a creamy whipped chocolate mousse! You can make this version plain chocolate or add mint to make it more gourmet and interesting. In just a few minutes, you can will have the best creamy chocolate mousse on the planet! The photo was taken before serving this dessert at my raw organic restaurant. Hopefully I will open a national chain soon, so everyone can enjoy it too!

THEME: AMERICAN | SERVINGS: 1–2

INGREDIENTS

1 Cup Raw Organic Pine Nuts

3 to 4 tablespoons Coconut Nectar

4 tablespoons Carob Powder

Handful Organic Mint Leaves

1/3 Cup Organic Coconut Oil (optional)

1/4 Cup Water

DIRECTIONS:

In the blender, first add the water then the other ingredients, so that it will blend.

Blend all the ingredients until super smooth and fluffy, and pour into a nice serving dish. Mousse can be chilled in the refrigerator or served right away. Garnish with some mint and your favorite fruit, and serve.

Peach Cobbler

Peach is one of my favorite fruits. You can truly taste summer in this delicious cobbler. The recipe does not require any machines or electricity, just with chopping and mixing by hand, making it real a Eco Chef recipe!

THEME: AMERICAN | SERVINGS: 2

INGREDIENTS

1 Large Organic Peach

1/3 Cup Organic Raisins

1/3 Cup Organic Walnuts and Organic Pecans

Dash Organic Cinnamon

Coconut Nectar to taste (or make your own sweetener by blending raisins or pitted dates with water)

Mint for garnish

DIRECTIONS:

Slice the peaches and put in serving bowl. Chop the walnuts and raisins, mix in a bowl with sweetener or coconut nectar. Sprinkle the peaches with cinnamon, garnish with mint and edible flowers (optional) and serve.

Make sure they are edible flowers!

Chocolate Chip Cookies

Imagine a chocolate chip cookie that only takes a few minutes to prepare. Well, imagine no more, because here it is, no bake tastes great! All your vitamins, minerals and healthy nutrition are still in each cookie. My most popular and requested dessert recipe.

THEME: AMERICAN | SERVINGS: 3–4

INGREDIENTS

1 Cup Raw Organic Almonds, soaked or not

1 Cup Water

2 Tablespoons Coconut Nectar

Dash of Organic Cinnamon

1 Cup Raw Organic Golden Flax Seeds, ground (or Flax USA pre-ground)

CHOCOLATE CHIPS:

1/3 Cup Carob Powder

3 to 4 Tablespoons Coconut Nectar

DIRECTIONS:

This recipe is for when you want to make a quick batch of about 8 chocolate cookies. You can use non-soaked almonds if you do not have soaked on hand, but soaked are better to make this a living cookie. This version is only if you do not have soaked almonds or almond pulp mixed with a sweetener ready.

Cookies: Pour water into the blender, add almonds and blend until almonds are a small crumb size. Pour into a cheesecloth, squeeze the almond milk into a bowl and set aside. Mix the almond pulp with coconut nectar and a dash of cinnamon.

Make small balls with your hands and flatten into cookie shapes, compacting to help them stick together. Coat with ground golden flax seeds and place on a plate.

Chocolate chips: Hand mix the coconut nectar with the carob powder, using more carob powder and less coconut nectar to

make the mixture firmer. Let it sit for a few minutes to firm up. Make "chocolate chips" with your hands or with two toothpicks or a spoon. Press down or lightly pat the "chocolate chips" on top of the cookie so they stay, and serve these moist and delicious Raw Living Super-Nutritious Chocolate Cookies.

You can have cookies and "milk," with the almond milk. Add carob powder and coconut nectar to the almond milk you will have "chocolate milk!"

Some people like to dehydrate the cookies in the Good4U Dehydrator at 114° for a few hours to make them more firm or dry. Always turn the temperature as high as you can at first, to eliminate the possibility of mold or fungus growth, then for the next ten minutes slowly reduce the temperature to 114°. All dehydrated foods should be prepared this way, as researched by Gabriel Cousens, MD.

The super energy really comes through in the great taste of this recipe. Can you imagine a sweet, decadent snack treat that is actually good for you, helping to anti-age and beautify you from the inside!? Well, it is real, and now you get to enjoy it. Kids really love these; you are providing them with the best food on the planet. Adults totally love these too, so make some for your friends and let them know the benefits. They will thank you for it. An innovative, organic, living superfood dessert!

Ginger Cookies

I loved ginger cookies as a kid, but this is a new, fresh, fun version that is all-natural and organic!

THEME: AMERICAN
SERVINGS: 3–4

INGREDIENTS

1 Cup Raw Organic Almonds, soaked (in water overnight in a covered bowl in a dry area) or non soaked

1 Cup Water

2 Tablespoons Coconut Nectar

2 Teaspoons Organic Ginger, fresh, finely grated

Dash Organic Cinnamon

1 Cup Raw Organic Golden Flax Seeds, ground (or FlaxUSA pre-ground)

DIRECTIONS:

This recipe works if you do not have prepared almond pulp mixed with coconut nectar on hand and you need to make a batch quickly. If you do not have soaked almonds ready, use raw almonds in the recipe.

If you have almond pulp mixed with coconut nectar on hand, simply mix in the grated ginger and cinnamon, coat with ground flaxseed on the outside, then compact and shape into cookies or make fun gingerbread shapes with cookie cutters.

To prepare the recipe, pour the water into the blender, add the almonds and blend until they are a very small crumb size. Pour into a cheesecloth and squeeze all the almond milk into a bowl. Set aside the almond milk.

Mix the almond pulp with coconut nectar, cinnamon and grated fresh ginger. Mix well with a fork, then make small balls with your hands and flatten into cookie shapes, compacting them to help them stick together. Coat with ground golden flax seeds and place on a serving plate. The cookies will be moist and delicious. Think of them as soft batches. You can even use the almond milk and have cookies and "milk." Makes 8 quick ginger cookies.

Banana Cream Pie

A classic favorite American dessert and a perfect way to enjoy a healthy fruit. This recipe is so quick and easy that it will become your favorite, too!

THEME: AMERICAN | SERVINGS: 2–3

INGREDIENTS

1 Organic Banana

1 Cup, your choice Raw Organic Nuts, soaked:
Sunflower Seeds
or Raw Organic Almonds
or Pine Nuts

1/4 Cup Coconut Nectar

1/4 Cup Water

PIE CRUST:

Almond Pulp (from Almond Milk)
1/4 cup Coconut Nectar

OR
1 Cup Pistachio Nuts, ground
1/4 Cup Coconut Nectar

OR
1 to 2 Cups Flax Seeds, ground
1 Banana

Garnish (optional)
Goji Berries, soaked and sliced
Banana

Organic Cinnamon to taste

DIRECTIONS:

This super-creamy Banana Cream Pie doesn't even need a crust. If you would like one, I recommend trying these different crusts:

- Pistachio nuts, ground to powder in the blender. Hand mix with coconut nectar or a sweetener made of raisins or pitted dates blended with water.
- Golden Flax Seeds, ground to powder in the blender

Hand mix with mashed banana and shaped into a crust. (see photo)

Press crust mixture into a single round glass serving bowl. To make a whole pie, triple this recipe.

Variation: Add a few tablespoons of carob powder to taste, to create a "chocolate crust."

Filling: Blend water, banana, coconut nectar, a few sprinkles of cinnamon and your choice of nuts until smooth. I have found that soaked sunflower seeds are the best for this recipe, but do try different nuts and combinations and expand your flavor palate.

Pour Banana Cream mixture into the crust. Garnish with soaked goji berries and slices of banana and sprinkle some cinnamon on top. Serve right away or let chill in the refrigerator for 10-30 minutes. Kids really love this one and I get plenty of requests for it.

Squeeze lemon on top to prevent the color from getting dark on top. The color will change very quickly, even if you put in the refrigerator. Try to serve this immediately or soon after making it. You can also scrape off a thin top layer before serving if you are storing it.

Note on Soaking Nuts: To soak the raw organic sunflower seeds just put in a covered bowl with clean water in a dry place over night, you don't have to soak them but the enzymes and nutrients becomes activated making it really healthy and it also makes digesting easier so it is worth soaking nuts and sprouting them when you can.

Note on Flax Seeds: Flax USA Pre-Groud Organic Golden Flax seeds are convenient, straight ofrom the package. They use a cold-milled process that allows nutrients to last much longer than if you grind them yourself, up to 22 months. When you grind them yourself, the nutrients are exposed to high temperatures, start to oxidize, and lose value instantly. Purchasing from Flax USA is a better, easier way to use golden flax seeds.

Tiramisu

Tiramisu is one of my favorite all-time desserts, so of course I had to come up with a amazing Raw Organic Vegan version that is even better and easier to make!

THEME: ITALIAN | SERVINGS: 2–3

INGREDIENTS

1 Fresh Young Coconut, meat carefully scraped out

1 Tablespoon Organic Virgin Coconut Oil

4 Tablespoons Coconut Nectar

1/4 Cup Water

1/2 Cup Raw Organic Pine Nuts or Sunflower Seeds

Soaked Almond Pulp from Almond Milk Recipe
1/4 Cup Coconut Nectar

OR
1/2 Cup Raw Organic Golden Flax Seeds, ground
1 Banana
1/4 Cup Coconut Nectar

Organic Cinnamon to taste

Raw Organic Carob Powder to taste

DIRECTIONS:

To make the Tiramisu, form 3 long cookies with the almond pulp-coconut nectar mixture. You can use 3 long slivers made of bananas instead.

Blend water, pine nuts or sunflower seeds with coconut nectar or sweetener that you make; add carob powder to taste, about 2 to 3 tablespoons is the suggested amount.

Spoon the first layer from the blender around the "cookies" and pat down with a spoon or your hands to make it firm.

Blend water, coconut meat, coconut oil, coconut nectar (or homemade sweetener of raisins or pitted dates blended with water) and carob powder. Blend until smooth, then pour over the Tiramisu, sprinkle some cinnamon and serve!

In the photograph I use fresh raw organic cranberries as a fun garnish.

Energy Bar

Make your own fresh, healthy, all-natural organic energy bar that will give you all the RAW energy you need!

THEME: ITALIAN | SERVINGS: 2–3

INGREDIENTS

1 Cup Raw Organic Sunflower Seeds

1 Cup Pumpkin Seeds

1 Cup Pine Nuts

1 Cup Almonds

1/4 Cup Raw Organic Buckwheat Groats, soaked in Water

1/2 Cup pitted Organic Dates, chopped into small pieces and mashed

Goji Berries to taste

DIRECTIONS:

These are great for snacks, hiking trips, and to have on hand for some quick, good. pick-me-up energy. For this recipe, I have found that using the nuts and seeds dry (not soaked) helps to keep them crunchy and they tend to hold together in the bars better. You do need to soak the buckwheat to soften.

Choose one or more of the first 5 ingredients to mix. (One of my favorite combinations is sunflower seed, pumpkin seed, dried goji berries and soaked buckwheat.) Combine your ingredients of choice in the blender or food processor for just a few seconds. (I recommend the Blendtec Blender because it is the most powerful.)

Mix nuts in a bowl with the pitted dates,, a little water, and some more whole dried goji berries, then shape and compact it enough that it stays together as an Energy Bar. The dates have a high sugar content, so use in moderation.

I like using the various cookie molds because you can compact them into fun shapes and they work really well. You can also make balls, using your hands or use a fork on a plate, to make really compacted Energy Bars. After shaping and compacting them, add more energy by allowing them to sit in direct sunlight for a while. Depending on how good you are at compacting and mixing these energy bars, they may or may not stay together, so you'll want to store them in containers when transporting.

As a side note, one of my favorite quick Trail Mixes is simply pine nuts with goji Berries. You can add other ingredients, of course, but I have found this mix to be satisfying, quick and easy. The creaminess of the pine nuts compliments the

sweetness of the goji berries. Often I will put a mix together in the morning and bring them with me as I head out for the day. It makes the perfect happy energy snack! Remember, goji berries are a "Superfood." I know that people will soon discover all the wonderful benefits of them, as I am helping to introduce them to people. They are so delicious and they really make you feel happy!

DESSERTS

Cookie Dough

Guilt-free snacking with this gourmet version of a junk food favorite. This recipe can be made in a variety of ways.

THEME: AMERICAN
SERVINGS: 4–5

INGREDIENTS

1 Jar Raw Organic Sprouted Macadamia Nut Butter
or regular Macadamia Nut Butter
(not mixed with Cashew)
or Raw Organic Tahini

3 to 4 Tablespoons Coconut Nectar

Few Sundried Organic Mulberries

Raw Organic Cacao Nibs to taste

DIRECTIONS:

If you can find the sprouted macadamia nut butter, that works best for this recipe. Next best is regular macadamianut butter, and the third alternative is raw organic tahini.

Simply spoon macadamia butter from the jar, stir in cacao nibs and sundried mulberries, and serve! Drizzle coconut nectar (optional) to sweeten it a little.

If you use regular macadamia butter, you may have to freeze it to make it firm and it may not stay hard or solid for long, especially if you live in a warm climate. In that case, use the next version!

Scoop tahini with a spoon into a mixing bowl and stir in the coconut nectar, cacao nibs and sundried mulberries, form into "Cookie Dough" balls and serve!

Put it on top of Raw Organic Ice Cream, eat as is, or serve next to your fruit smoothie. Macadamia butter and tahini are both healthy and nutritious. Once again, a favorite junk food recipe is now transformed into the most healthy recipe in the world!

Green Tea Pistachio
Ice Cream

This is a super-simple, unique Asian Fusion Five-Star Raw Spa new recipe! Using organic green tea and pistachios, you are making fine Eco Green Cuisine! Asian Fusion recipes and cuisine are very popular in all Five-Star Spas and Resorts around the world; many are located in Asia or Southeast Asia as well.

THEME: JAPANESE | SERVINGS: 4–5

INGREDIENTS

Organic Green Tea, loose or in a teabag

3 Cups Pure Water

2 Cups Raw Organic Pistachios, shelled

5 to 6 Tablespoons Coconut Nectar

DIRECTIONS:

Soak the green tea in room temperature or warm water to the desired level of flavor. Pour into the blender, adding the water, pistachios and coconut nectar, and blend until smooth. Pour into a freezer-safe bowl and freeze overnight until solid.

The next day, carefully take out of the freezer and scrape with a fork pressure (see photo). When you've scraped enough Ice Cream, use a spoon or ice cream scoop to make scoops, and serve. Mix coconut nectar with carob powder to make a "Chocolate Sauce" and drizzle on top, adding your favorite berries. Green tea has fantastic antioxidants and benefits. Serve on a hot day and enjoy!

You can easily make other flavors in this manner too, such as strawberry, etc. Experiment with different fruit, combinations and variations. Be creative and have fun!

Carrot Cake

It's carrot and cake, a favorite combination, and now the Raw Organic Living version, the no-bake-tastes-great Carrot Cake!

THEME: AMERICAN | SERVINGS: 4–5

INGREDIENTS

1 Cup Soaked Almond Pulp from Almond Milk (Oatmeal Cereal recipe)

OR

2 Cups Pistachio Nuts or Pecans

OR

1 to 2 Cups Golden Flax Seeds
1 banana

CAKE:

2 Large grated Organic Carrots

1/4 Cup Coconut Nectar

1/2 Cup Water

Cinnamon to taste

2 Cups Soaked Almond Pulp

FROSTING:

1/2 Cup Raw Organic Pine Nuts

2 to 3 Tablespoons Raw Organic Coconut Oil

1/4 Cup Water

3 Tablespoons Coconut Nectar

Organic Cinnamon to taste

DIRECTIONS:

In the Blendtec Blender (you can use other blenders, but I really recommend the Blendtec for its power and performance in making my recipes), add pistachios and blend until a crumb size. Pour into a bowl and mix with coconut nectar until well mixed. Press into a glass pie pan, shape into a crust and set aside.

Variations:

- 1 to 2 cups soaked almond pulp (from Almond Milk recipe) mixed with 1/4 cup coconut nectar

- 1 to 2 cups golden flax seeds ground to powder and hand mixed with mashed banana

- 1 to 2 cups of sunflower seeds ground to powder and mixed with 1/4 cup coconut nectar

- Add a few tablespoons of carob powder to taste when blending or mixing to make a "chocolate" pie crust!

In the blender add the water first, then Brazil nuts, chopped mango and coconut nectar, and blend until smooth. Pour the Mango Cheesecake mix over the crust and serve right away, or chill until firm. Garnish with sliced strawberries or soaked goji berries for a colorful gourmet presentation.

FROSTING VARIATION: Coat the top of the cake with raw organic coconut oil and drizzle coconut nectar to taste for a fast, simple "frosting." Add grated carrots for garnish. (see photo)

Mango "Cheesecake"

Everyone loves my world famous Raw Organic Mango "Cheesecake," which has no cheese or dairy yet is creamier than any cheesecake out there! This colorful, vibrant dessert is an amazing crowd pleaser; the bright yellow vegan version will cheer up all "cheesecake" fans. "Vegan" is now hip, trendy, desirable, and also practical, eco, healthy, fashionable and fun. Give this recipe a try; I guarantee it will change your mind and views about Raw Organic Vegan foods. I have had people tell me this was the best dessert they ever had. Please make sure all the ingredients are Raw and Organic.

THEME: AMERICAN | SERVINGS: 4–5,

INGREDIENTS

1 Large Organic Mango

1 1/2 Cups Raw Organic Brazil Nuts

1/4 Cup Coconut Nectar

1/2 Cup Water, or 1/3 for thicker consistency

1 Cup Raw Organic Pistachio Nuts

DIRECTIONS:

In the Blendtec Blender (you can use other blenders, but I really recommend the Blendtec for its power and performance in making my recipes), add pistachios and blend until a crumb size. Pour into a bowl and mix with coconut nectar until well mixed. Press into a glass pie pan, shape into a crust and set aside.

Variations:

- 1 to 2 cups soaked almond pulp (from Almond Milk recipe) mixed with 1/4 cup coconut nectar
- 1 to 2 cups golden flax seeds ground to powder and hand mixed with mashed banana
- 1 to 2 cups of sunflower seeds ground to powder and mixed with 1/4 cup coconut nectar
- Add a few tablespoons of carob powder to taste when blending or mixing to make a "chocolate" pie crust!

In the blender add the water first, then Brazil nuts, chopped mango and coconut nectar, and blend until smooth. Pour the Mango Cheesecake mix over the crust and serve right away, or chill until firm. Garnish with sliced strawberries or soaked goji berries for a colorful gourmet presentation.

This "cheesecake" is so colorful and delicious! Brazil nuts grow only in the rainforest and have great healing powers, enzymes, vitamins and minerals.

Open Face "Peanut Butter" Cups

Based on a classic "junk food" dessert, this recipe now is transformed into the world's most healthy, refreshing, Five Star Raw Spa Cuisine special recipe! You CAN enjoy "junk food" that is now all natural and actually really good for you, with maximum nutrition, vitamins, minerals and many RAWmazing benefits! Instead of peanuts we use Raw Organic Almond Butter, which has more benefits, more nutrition, and better flavor and texture too!

THEME: AMERICAN | SERVINGS: 4–5

INGREDIENTS

1 Organic Gala Apple

4 to 5 Tablespoons Raw Organic Almond Butter

5 Tablespoons Coconut Nectar

1/3 Cup Carob Powder

Organic Berries and Mint for garnish (optional)

DIRECTIONS:

Using a knife to carefully slice even, thin slices of apple and place on a serving plate. To make the "Chocolate Sauce," mix the carob powder with coconut nectar in a bowl (or make your own sweetener by blending raisins or pitted dates with water). Put a spoonful of sauce on each slice of apple.

Place a spoonful of Almond butter atop each "Chocolate Sauce" (see photo). Garnish with your favorite berry and mint. You can serve as is, or drizzle a little more coconut nectar, then serve.

This is a great example of Five Star Raw Spa Cuisine: simple, elegant, fast, easy yet super nutritious and RAWmazingly RAWlicious! The point of Raw Organic Cuisine is to fully benefit from alkalizing your body, maintaining a neutral Ph, hydration, oxygen and the benefits from your food choices. Raw Organic food keeps the active enzymes, nutrition, vitamins and minerals intact and does not have high acrylamide levels; please look up these terms and health principles to learn more.

Note: New coconut nectar is very healthy, with no sugar, low glycemic index, neutral Ph and living enzymes. You will feel amazingly healthy after trying it just once! Available on my online store.

Chocolate Dipping Sauce

Everyone loves chocolate covered strawberries! Now you can make it at home easily. I make this recipe at celebrity events or fancy parties and it is a real crowd pleaser. You can use this easy chocolate sauce for dipping strawberries, pitted cherries, bananas…and for just about anything that you like to serve with chocolate sauce, like a banana split. What you can do with this recipe is unlimited, and best of all it takes 5 minutes or less to make!

THEME: ITALIAN | SERVINGS: 2–3

INGREDIENTS

3 Tablespoons Raw Organic Carob Powder

4 Tablespoons Coconut Nectar

A new variation calls for using fresh coconut water from a real coconut in place of the nectar. Mix a few tablespoons with the carob powder until you reach the desired thickness and consistency. A new low sugar, low calorie treat!

DIRECTIONS:

Mix by hand, then dip or coat, serve with strawberries or on top of desserts!

ENTIRELY NEW

ENTIRELY NEW BY ECO CHEF BRYAN AU : FRUIT DESSERT RECIPES & CATEGORY

These recipes are totally new innovative 100% Raw Organic fruit dessert versions of savory classic dishes and recipes. They can be served as an appetizer or entrée but work best as a surprise dessert.

"Shrimp"

A totally new Eco Chef Special Category: Fruit Dessert recipes that look like classic seafood. Another Eco Chef innovation, and a fun recipe to try. A friend of mine asked if I had a Raw Organic "Shrimp" recipe, and this is the closest that I can come to a Raw, Organic, plant based "Shrimp." The theme of Raw Organic Vegan Cuisine stretches my creativity to invent new recipes and techniques. It is challenging and fun at the same time, one of the reasons millions of people are drawn to Raw Organic Cuisine. The new tastes, textures and flavors and the assortment of new recipes also makes it unique, interesting and one of the most fun cuisines to come along in a long time. It is a true food revolution, and I am so happy that you are joining the adventure with me!

THEME: AMERICAN | SERVINGS: 3–4

INGREDIENTS

1 Organic Gala or Fuji Apple

2 or 3 Sundried Organic Apricots

DIRECTIONS:

Peel the apple and cut into wedges. Using a RAW STAR 4" Ceramic Knife, carefully cut and carve a sundried apricot to make shrimp like shapes, put on top of the apple and serve. Please use the photo as a guide.

This can be served as an appetizer, entree, snack or dessert. For a "Shrimp Cocktail Sauce" in keeping with the fruit and dessert, crush some organic strawberries and serve alongside this new dessert!

Note: The RAW STAR 4" Ceramic Knife has a special point in order to carve fruits and vegetables. Some ceramic knives have a round or curved point, making this task impossible, but RAW STAR Ceramic Knives are designed to make you a Star in the kitchen!

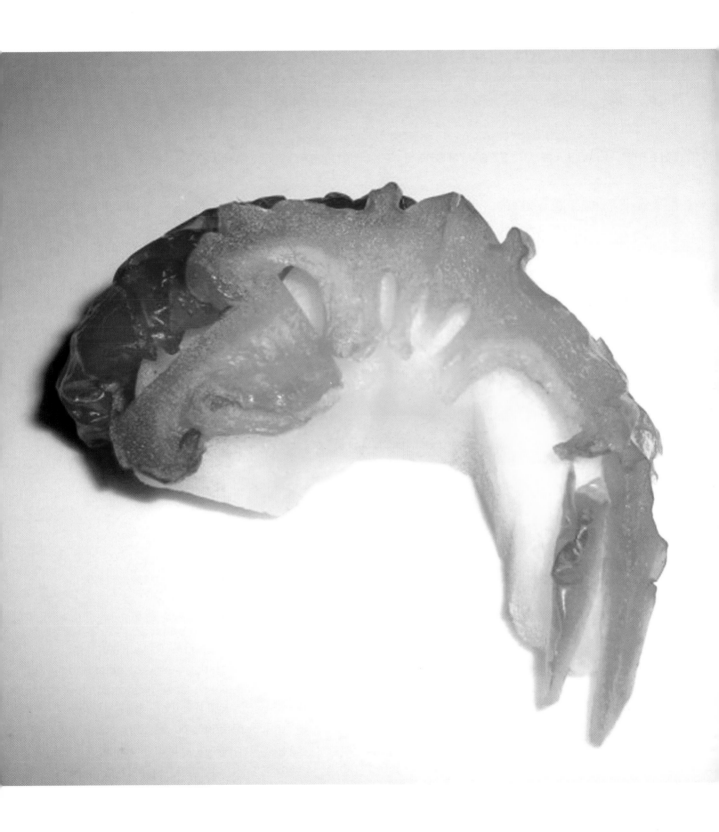

Fruit Penne Mango "Pasta"

A totally new Eco Chef Special Category of Fruit Desserts that look like classic savory dishes and can be served as an appetizer, entree or dessert. Raw Organic Cuisine is so new and cutting edge that you can be delighted and dazzled with totally new flavors, recipes, and of course, desserts!

THEME: ITALIAN | SERVINGS: 1–2

INGREDIENTS

1 to 2 Organic Mangoes

2 Organic Strawberries

1 Organic Asian Pear

Few Organic Mint Leaves

Note: Conventional stainless steel or metal peelers will just make a mess, but RAW STAR Ceramic Peelers glide perfectly and work great!

DIRECTIONS:

Start by thinly slicing the mangoes using the RAW STAR Ceramic Peeler. Make thin slices with the Ceramic Peeler and "score" one side with a fork, or make shallow, slicing cuts for the outside of the "Penne Pasta." Roll them up and cut each end on an angle. Chop strawberries into cubes to become the "tomatoes," then slice an Asian pear into sliver like shapes for the melted "parmesan cheese." Chop mint for "parsley" and serve! This is delicious and a really pretty dessert, and can also be served as an appetizer or entree.

Fruit "Sushi" Rolls, or "Frushi"

It is a really cute and smart recipe made with mango as the "seaweed" and banana and raspberries as the "fruit sushi" middle. You can use my Ceramic Peeler to make the mango slices necessary f or this fun and colorful recipe!

THEME: JAPANESE
SERVINGS: 5–6

INGREDIENTS

1 Fresh Organic Mango

1 Organic Banana

1 Fresh Organic Strawberry or other berry

1 Organic Green Apple

DIRECTIONS:

Peel the Mango using my RAW STAR Ceramic Peeler, then use the peeler to create long flat slices, carefully and slowly; if you have really good knife skills, you can use the Ceramic Knife to carefully make uniformly thick, long "sheets" of mango to roll up the "Fruit Sushi."

When you have enough slices or "sheets" of mango, place them on a plate. Peel the banana and cut small sushi sized pieces that will become the middle of the "Fruit Sushi." Carefully wrap each banana piece with mango; you can trim it with a knife, but be very careful not to cut yourself! Cut apple and strawberry and place on top, garnish with mint or edible organic flowers (optional, available in stores or health food stores). To make the "ginger," slice apple pieces and crush some strawberry to stain or color it pink. Grate green apple skin to make the "wasabi."

Fruit "Cheeseburger & Fries"

This is a world's first 100% Raw Organic Vegan "Cheeseburger and Fries" made out of 100% Raw Organic Fruit! Very fun and whimsical recipe that actually tastes really good too. For fun see if you can guess what the fruit being used is in this recipe.

THEME: AMERICAN | SERVINGS: 1–2

INGREDIENTS

1 Asian Pear = Bun

1 Coconut = Mayo

Mint = Lettuce

Sliced Mango = Cheddar Cheese

1 Each: Dried Fig, Dates, Raisins = Burger with grill marks

1 Slice of Watermelon = Tomato

Few Crushed Strawberries = Ketchup

Slice of Honeydew Melon = Pickles

Chopped Asian Pear = Fries

DIRECTIONS

Cut each fruit into the corresponding shape (see photo) like a round slice, thin slice or "fries" and serve!

Need a slice or a little of each fruit? Try using my Raw Star Ceramic Knife for precision cuts and to keep the fruit fresher longer. These recipes demonstrate the power of my RAW STAR Ceramic Knives. I would not be able to make these using metal or stainless steel knives, and the fruit would not stay as fresh and would wilt faster. My Ceramic Knives are the best new technology, must have knives in every kitchen, backed by a full lifetime guarantee and warranty. Good equipment really makes a difference!

Thai Coconut "Rice"

This is a very fancy and refreshing dish, best served during the spring or summer months, when it is warmer outside.

THEME: THAI | SERVINGS: 5–6

INGREDIENTS

1 Coconut

1 Organic Orange plus zest

1 Avocado

1 Bunch Organic Cilantro

Organic Ginger, grated

Sea Salt to taste

Chopped Mint Leaves

Lime juice to taste

DIRECTIONS:

Carefully open a fresh coconut; scrape out the meat. Chop by hand or use a grater to make tiny rice like pieces. Place into a large serving bowl, chop the avocado, orange and mint, and toss on top of the coconut "rice." Grate the ginger on top, season with sea salt. Sprinkle the lime juice on top and serve with cilantro as garnish.

Fruit "Steak Dinner with Mashed Potato, Mushroom & Gravy"

This is a fun and novel recipe made entirely of 100% Raw Organic fruit! For fun, try to guess which fruits are used in this recipe.

THEME: AMERICAN | SERVINGS: 1–2

INGREDIENTS

1 Organic Banana

1 Slice Organic Watermelon

Organic Mango, half

3 to 4 Organic Dates, pitted

White part of Organic Grapefruit

DIRECTIONS:

Cut a watermelon slice into a steak like shape and place on a serving plate. Mash pitted dates together in your hand and top the watermelon slice to make it look like a "steak." Cut a date in half to make two "mushroom tops" and slice the banana to make the mushroom stems (see photo). Smash the rest of the banana and form a "mashed potato" shape, using your hands. Use dates for "gravy" on top of the banana "mashed potato." The corn is half of the mango on the skin, cut into corn like pieces, and the "butter" is the white part of a grapefruit. It actually tastes great, too!

Fruit "Fried Crab Wontons"

This is a easy and fun fruit dessert with a dipping sauce of its own. It's very light, colorful and refreshing as a appetizer, snack or entrée, but best as a dessert.

THEME: CHINESE | SERVINGS: 3–4

INGREDIENTS

1 Organic Fuji or Gala Apple

2 to 3 Sundried Apricots

1 Organic Banana

1 Organic Lemon or Lime, juiced

2 Organic Strawberries

A chunk of Organic Honey Dew Melon and Cantaloupe for garnish

1 Sprig Organic Mint for garnish

DIRECTIONS:

Slice the apple as thinly as thin as possible, then cut into triangle shapes (see photo). Slice the apricots into thin matchstick shapes. Peel and mash the banana in a medium mixing bowl, add the sliced apricots and hand mix well. Sprinkle either the lemon or lime juice on top.

Using a spoon, place the banana apricot mixture into the middle of each sliced apple, then add another triangle sliced apple piece on top, as in the photo. Mash strawberries to make a "dipping sauce" in a small dipping bowl. Grate or slice the chunk of honeydew melon and cantaloupe for a garnish; serve with mint and enjoy a totally new, refreshing and colorful dish.

Chocolate Shake

A frothy "milky" creamy chocolate shake with no chocolate in it! We use Raw Organic Carob Powder instead. Chocolate lovers will celebrate with this recipe!

THEME: AMERICAN | SERVINGS: 2

INGREDIENTS

1 Fresh Young Coconut, flesh and water, OR 1 1/2 Cups Almond Milk OR other nut milk

4 Tablespoons Carob Powder

2 to 3 Tablespoons Coconut Nectar

DIRECTIONS:

Carefully scrape the coconut flesh. Pour the coconut water into a bowl, take out the splinters and fibers, then pour into the blender and add thecarob powder and coconut nectar. Blend to desired consistency. If you do not have access to fresh young coconuts then you can use almond milk or other nut milk. This is one vegan Chocolate Shake that is so super creamy and amazing.

Cosmic Green Smoothie

Every Five Star Spa serves a Green Smoothie that is very healthy, refreshing, alkalizing and more. I have one nearly every morning, and I know many people who enjoy them as a healthy, fast, breakfast on-the-go.;I found this recipe to be the most RAWmazing, after I drank it I felt instantly at ONE with the entire Universe and I actually felt it working through my body in a healthy way. It is so healthy that you have to experience this for yourself!

THEME: AMERICAN | SERVINGS: 2

INGREDIENTS

Bunch Organic Dandelion Greens (bitter, detox, super green; helps rejuvenate kidney and liver. Get them from a health food store, most Whole Foods Markets carry them)

1 Bunch Organic Dino Kale (Super green! Some people do not usually eat, but it's perfect in a green smoothie)

1 Lime (activate enzymes and energy)

1/3 Cup Pineapple (increases digestion, flavor, optional but good!)

Some goji berry (Happy!)

A few spoonfuls Organic Coconut oil (just a little for anti-aging effects)

1 Organic Avocado (makes it creamy and benefits too! Optional)

1 Organic Banana (sweetness and flavor to balance the bitter greens)

1 Organic Orange (flavor and vitamin C)

Touch of Coconut Nectar (energy and sweet)

1 Kombucha (anti-radiation, anti-emf, anti-aging)

Cayenne Pepper (increases digestion and circulation)

Spicy hot pepper (increases digestion and circulation)

Organic Broccoli Sprouts (bitter, detox. I read that eating the sprouts is more nutritious than eating the florets)

2 Cups Water   adjust to desired thickness of smoothie

DIRECTIONS:

Blend all ingredients until smooth, then enjoy and feel the bliss!

Strawberry Goji Berry Shake

Why not make your own fresh, wholesome, totally organic all natural strawberry smoothies, just the way you like, and with organic raw goji berries? This is superfood!

THEME: AMERICAN | SERVINGS: 2

INGREDIENTS

1 Fresh Young Coconut

1 Cup Fresh Organic Strawberries chopped into small pieces

2 Tablespoons Coconut Nectar

1/4 Cup soaked Goji Berries

DIRECTIONS:

Carefully scrape the coconut flesh. Pour the coconut water into a bowl, take out all the splinters and fibers, then pour into the blender, adding the rest of the ingredients. Add a few goji berries before blending to give this smoothie its nice color. Blend to desired consistency. If you do not have access to fresh young coconuts, try almond milk instead. This is a really great refreshing island style drink.

Goji berries give this smoothie a vibrant, unique, energetic flavor that will delight you while giving you amazing super vitality. I know that the more people discover and try goji berries, the more blissed out they will become! Bliss is one of my favorite yoga terms. According to yoga, bliss and joy is our all natural state of being, and ultimately our real true self. That is why the Raw Organic Living Cuisine is the best diet and choice for returning to our true, healthy identity and state of well being.

Variations: Add 1/2 cup of strawberries before blending for a great mix. Try pineapple or honeydew melon too.

Just a reminder that pineapple and honeydew melons are considered to be high glycemic and high sugar index fruit. We use them sparingly in my recipes. Pineapple has such amazing digestive live enzyme qualities that I like to use it and include it in recipes. It also has great flavor and the Island Vibe. The best pineapples I have found come from Maui, Hawaii.

Almond "Milk" Recipe

Raw Organic vegan version of milk that is creamy, delicious, healthy and nutritious! Vegan is now delicious, desirable, hip, trendy and fashionable. Raw organic almonds happens to be the #1 most nutritional nut in the world. Avoid the hormones and pesticides in dairy and enjoy the pure, refreshing, wholesome "Milk" that is truly good for you.

The point of Raw Organic Cuisine is to enjoy the best, most gourmet, pure food and reap the benefits of what Raw Organic food can do for you. You have to discover it for yourself; you will want to go further with it, as millions of people have. We want the world to enjoy it and discover the amazing adventure too.

Try something new that is good for you and for the planet while being the fun, fashionable and delicious! You literally will be "SAVING EVERYTHING," which is my new motto! Experience a whole new level of health, well being, clarity, joy, happiness, energy, anti-aging, and so many wonderful benefits that you can see and feel instantly.

THEME: AMERICAN | SERVINGS: 2

INGREDIENTS

3 Cups Almonds (soaked or not, but soaked is better)

4 Cups Water

1/4 Cup Coconut Nectar

For a smaller batch:

2 Cups of Almonds (Soaked or not)

3 Cups of Water

Few Tablespoons of Coconut Nectar

DIRECTIONS:

You can use non-soaked almonds if you do not have any soaked, but it is better to have soaked ones in which the vitamins, minerals, nutrition and enzymes are active and alive, for maximum health benefits and well being! A easy way to do it is to soak the almonds overnight before you go to sleep; when you wake up, they are ready to use. Make sure that you rinse the almonds in clean, pure water, and never use the soaking water.

Add fresh water to the blender and add the almonds. Blend until they are a very small crumb size. Pour into a cheesecloth or strainer, squeeze the almond milk into a bowl, and set aside the almond milk. Place the almond pulp into a separate bowl for use in making cookies, pie crusts and other recipes. Pour the "milk" into your favorite eco recycled drinking glass, serve and enjoy!

WINE PAIRING

This page and section is strictly for ADULTS ONLY ABOVE AGE 21 because of the Alcohol Information. This Section and pages are not for kids or children.

As part of being a Eco Chef, I enjoy recommending new, healthy and environmentally friendly information for people to benefit from. We all have a lot of power and our daily choices really do directly affect our health, well being and the entire world. By making the best choices we can all improve our health, community and planet together in the most fun, fashionable and delicious ways possible.

One new important fact that I would like to share with you has to do with organic wines. Bonterra Organic Wines from Mendocino are my favorite. They have been growing organic grapes and making wine since 1987. Their motto is "Organic grapes make for better wine." I strongly agree, and add that it also makes for better health and a better world as well!

That is shocking news for a lot of people but it is true; if you do your own research, there is a lot of information online about this. Wine is something that many people enjoy and is healthy in moderation. Now we can choose the best organic wine, thanks to Bonterra Vineyards. Visit their website at www.Bonterra. com.

I truly appreciate that they take the extra time, care and costs in order to save our health and environment! So thank you, Bonterra, for caring and providing us with the best choice, quality, price and flavor in organic wines! This is a quote from their Website and I would like to share it with you:

"Why grow grapes organically? It's good for the earth and great for taste.

At Bonterra, we take our cues from the land and the fruit. We let them tell us what to do.

Our holistic approach to winemaking took root in 1987 when we were experimenting with wine and food pairings. The fruits, vegetables and herbs we used came from our extensive organic garden. The purity, intensity and freshness of the flavors were amazing. From that point on, we committed ourselves to growing grapes organically.

Over the years, we've evolved our philosophy based on what we know works. Today our vineyard is an environment of incredible diversity: soil, plants and animals work together to create a web of natural balance where all the elements thrive.

Decades of learning and winemaking accolades have reinforced our passionate belief that our organic grapes make better wine."

If you are ever in the Mendocino, CA area, stop by their winery and visit! They are the nicest people and family I have ever met. They offer great wine tastings, samples and more.

In honor of their dedication and award-winning wines, I have dedicated this section to include WINE PAIRINGS with Bonterra Organic Wines.

RAW Star Recipes	Wine Flavors	Food Affinities	Bonterra Organic Chardonnay
Spinach Herb Dip, "Shrimp", Pasta Alfredo, Fruity "Tuna" Wraps, Onion Rings, Mango "Cheesecake," Baklava, "Clam" Chowder, "Sushi," Fruit "Sushi," Cucumber Honeydew Melon Soup	Green apple Baked apple Pear Lemon zest Vanilla	Almonds Fresh sage Tarragon Orange zest Lemon zest	

RAW Star Recipes	Wine Flavors	Food Affinities	Bonterra Organic Sauvignon Blanc
"Chicken and Turkey," Holiday Stuffing, "Shrimp," Thai Coconut Soup, Goji Macaroons	Grapefruit Gooseberry Lemongrass Kiwi Melon Guava	Lemon Citrus Basil Lemon thyme Lemon verbena Mint Cilantro Tarragon Chevre Chives Green olives	

RAW Star Recipes	Wine Flavors	Food Affinities	Bonterra Organic Viogner
"Shrimp," Pad Thai, Thai Coconut Soup, Tacos, Hawaiian Pizza, Fruity "Tuna" Wraps, Waldorf Salad, Peach Cobbler	Peaches & cream Jasmine Honeysuckle Apricot Touch of vanilla	Rich triple crème cheeses such as D'Affinois Dried apricots Dried peaches Lemongrass Coconut milk Mild yellow curry	

RAW Star Recipes	Wine Flavors	Food Affinities	Bonterra Organic Zinfandel
"Steak," "Meat" Loaf, Raspberry Chocolate Cinnamon Crumb Cake, 5 Minute Chocolate Cake, Triple Layer Chocolate Cake	Red raspberry Brambly blackberry White and black pepper Rich plum	Pepper Oregano Cinnamon Clove Sage Lavender	

RAW Star Recipes	Wine Flavors	Food Affinities	Bonterra Organic Syrah
"Chicken and Turkey," Pad Thai, Super Nachos	Heady aromas of wild blackberry Bittersweet chocolate Vanilla Cedar spice	White pepper Cardamom Bay leaf Juniper Red mole Dark chocolate Licorice	

RAW Star Recipes	Wine Flavors	Food Affinities	Bonterra Organic Merlot
Yam Fries with Chili "Cheese," Samosas, Holiday Stuffing, Sloppy Joes, Falafel, Blueberry Mousse Pie with Graham Crust	Blackberry Cherry Touches of herbs Cedar	Tomato Vanilla Tea Soy Anise Clove Mint Rosemary	

RAW Star Recipes	Wine Flavors	Food Affinities	Bonterra Organic Cabarnet Sauvignon
"Pepperoni Pizza," Spanish Lasagna, "Steak," Super Nachos, Macaroni and Cheese	Bing Cherry Currents Raspberry Vanilla Spicy notes of cedar	Black olive Pesto Dark bittersweet chocolate Rosemary Mint Dried cherry	

Thank you for joining in the
Raw Organic Cuisine Adventure!
I hope you enjoyed my recipes. Please
share with loved ones, friends and family.

Now you are the RAW STAR!

Eco Chef Bryan Au